WORLDS
APART

D0107748

WORLDS APART

THE UNHOLY WAR BETWEEN RELIGION AND SCIENCE

KARL GIBERSON

Beacon Hill Press of Kansas City
Kansas City, Missouri

Copyright 1993
by Beacon Hill Press of Kansas City

ISBN: 083-411-5042

Printed in the
United States of America

Cover Design: Ted Ferguson
Cover Photo: Eric Curry/H. Armstrong Roberts

Unless otherwise indicated, all Scripture quotations are from the *Holy Bible, New International Version®* (NIV®). Copyright © 1973, 1978, 1984 by International Bible Society. Used by permission of Zondervan Publishing House. All rights reserved.

Scripture marked RSV is from the *Revised Standard Version of the Bible,* copyrighted 1946, 1952, © 1971, 1973. Used by permission.

KJV—King James Version

10   9   8   7   6   5   4   3   2   1

In memory of my grandfather,
Karl C. Steeves (September 24, 1901—May 27, 1979),
whose love of nature and a good book
was passed on to my mother.
And to my mother, who has passed these cherished gifts
on to me.
May I be as successful with my children.

CONTENTS

FOREWORD

The relation between religion and science has been an uneasy one since about the 16th century. One by one the new discoveries of science called into question long-held traditions about the natural world. Unfortunately, the Church had sanctified certain of these traditions with the result that it attempted to defend them with ecclesiastical authority. The consequence of these tragic chapters in history was considerable loss of credibility for the Church.

Mainstream theologians, subsequently, have been quite reticent to make pronouncements about scientific matters. There have always been those, however, who were not at all hesitant about going outside their field, usually with a great deal of dogmatism. The world at large simply passes by these people as eddies alongside the flow of the history of ideas.

Wesleyan theologians have identified more with the mainstream than the eddy waters. Both A. M. Hills and H. Orton Wiley found no problem with acknowledging the findings of modern science as not conflicting with biblical truth, including geological findings about the age of the earth. The standard statement in Wesleyan literature is that science and theology can never be in conflict when each remains within its proper domain. This proclamation has always been made by theologians and biblical scholars. For the first time, we have in this book a public attempt made by a Nazarene scientist to address the issue. Dr. Karl Giberson is a physicist who teaches at Eastern Nazarene College and writes with a burning desire that his discipline be allowed the freedom to follow its own canons of truth without being restricted by theologians who are not trained scientists. Hence, he addresses strongly and effectively the movement that seeks to foist religion upon the scientific community as if it were a science.

Since this is such an emotion-laden issue, Dr. Giberson has manifested a great deal of bravery in speaking out. He is not alone in this, however, since many trained evangelical scientists are vigorously doing the same thing, along with trained theologians and biblical scholars.

The danger of such a treatment as this is that it must, of necessity, address issues that the average person is not trained to comprehend. As a theologian, I am completely lost in discussions of quantum mechanics, theories of relativity, and supernovas. That is not my field. Tragically, too many do not accept such limitations, rejecting ideas they do not understand, often with much emotional fervor, even at times attacking the persons of those with whom they do not agree. Ignorance is not sin, but it can be a serious obstacle to the advancement of learning and productive of much animosity.

I was sitting one Sunday morning some years ago in a Sunday School class in a rural church while waiting for the morning service where I was scheduled to preach. It was soon after NASA had landed a man on the moon. One lady in the class protested that this was all a hoax. She argued that they had just made that stuff up and showed those fabricated pictures on television to fool us. While this is certainly an extreme case, it reflects a mind-set that is widespread in relation to science. This kind of mentality in the church makes it difficult to get at truth without disturbing a few people, but that should not become a deterrent to the Church allowing scholars to follow their disciplines without being smothered by uninformed opinion.

My own approach would be somewhat different from Dr. Giberson's in relating Genesis to modern science, even though the end result might be much the same. I would concur with W. H. Griffith Thomas, a revered conservative scholar, who said of Genesis 1 that "the truest method of comparison is not between this chapter and the results of modern science, but rather between this chapter and all other ancient cosmogonies."[1]

Relatively recent discoveries have demonstrated a close connection between the cosmology found in Genesis and that found in earlier Babylonian documents. This fact makes it problematic to speak of a revealed science. Thus, what we have in Genesis is a profoundly inspired theological interpretation of

---

1. *Genesis—A Devotional Commentary* (Grand Rapids: William B. Eerdmans Publishing Co., 1946), 30.

the prevailing science in the ancient world, a cosmology that has been long since outmoded. It may or may not have affinities with modern scientific theories, but that is a moot point. What is important is the theological dimension that has enduring relevance and authority. One of the positive values of this book is its distinction between the proper domain of theology and the proper domain of natural science.

What Dr. Giberson presents to us is not a declaration of independence from religion but a plea on the part of a dedicated Christian scientist, committed to the Lordship of Jesus Christ, that we not confuse the two disciplines, as is so often done on the popular level. What he has to say deserves careful study and consideration along with informed, thoughtful response.

—H. RAY DUNNING
Trevecca Nazarene College
Nashville

PREFACE

On the great fundamentals we are all agreed. Pertaining to things not essential to salvation, we have liberty. To attempt to emphasize that which is not essential to salvation, and thus to divide forces, would be a crime. An unwillingness for others to enjoy the liberty that we enjoy in reference to doctrines not vital to salvation is bigotry, from which the spirit of holiness withdraws itself.

Phineas F. Bresee

The quote above is the counsel of a wise man whose wisdom was informed by a profound spirituality. It is a wisdom that should animate all Christians as they confront disagreement among their Christian brothers and sisters. It is a wisdom that could solve many of the problems confronting the evangelical church today as the religious headlines speak sadly of schisms and discord among the Church of Jesus Christ, a church whose signature is supposed to be love. And it is a wisdom that came to me far too late.

When I arrived as a freshman at Eastern Nazarene College, I had been fully and of my own free will brainwashed into believing that modern science was a Satanic conspiracy. I had been misled by the many books I had read in the field of science and religion that had convinced me, with far more conviction than any high school student should legitimately acquire, that the cause of Christ was best served by pointing out to everyone that the modern theories of origins put forth by an unbelieving scientific community were incompatible with their faith. I argued vigorously with everyone, to absolutely no avail, and accomplished absolutely nothing, except perhaps to sow some seeds of discord.

I have called this struggle in which I was once entangled "the unholy war between religion and science." It is unholy because it creates discord with the kingdom of God as Christians lose sight of their essential unity and break ranks over superficial issues. It is unholy because it leads Christians to insult the integrity of scientists who have dedicated their lives to studying creation. It is unholy because it leads scientists to insult the integrity of Christians who have dedicated their lives to establishing a relationshp with the Creator. The tragedy is that there need be no conflict at all. It is only when we fail to understand the deeper issues that we can be persuaded that there is a conflict. But these deeper issues have roots that lie buried in previous centuries, in modes of thought long discarded, in perspectives unconsciously assumed, and in Sunday School lessons long forgotten.

Today I teach students who are struggling with these questions. Their term papers reveal the same tension that once pulled at my soul, the same uneasiness about how to respond to the challenges that modern science was laying at the feet of their cherished Christian faith. Many of them have emerged from a religious background like mine—one that leads them to divorce themselves from the contemporary world of science, believing that this is the calling of their faith.

I have written this book for my students, hopefully to help them avoid some of the snares that once entangled me.

My training is in physics, philosophy, and mathematics, and I have always had a strong layman's interest in theology and biblical studies. I have tried to draw on this diverse educational background in the framing of the argument that unfolds in the pages that follow. I am not a specialist in any field save atomic physics, and thus I cannot claim expertise in all of the various fields on which I have drawn to produce this book. But broad questions that cut across the disciplines cannot be left to the specialists. In fact, in the pages that follow I will argue that much of the intellectual mess in which we find ourselves today is the direct result of excessive professional specialization—the unfortunate tendency on the part of our modern university system to produce theologically illiterate scientists and scientifically illiterate theologians.

The reader must judge whether my argument succeeds, whether the following pages unfold naturally into a fan to produce a cooling breeze—or whether they should be crumpled and thrown onto the fire!

ACKNOWLEDGMENTS

The writing of this book—my first, but hopefully not my last—has been one of the most enjoyable experiences of my academic career. It is thus a pleasure to acknowledge the people who encouraged me, pushed me, steered me, and corrected me as the manuscript unfolded.

The recognition of a need for a book like this grew out of discussion among the science faculty from several Christian colleges at a conference in 1988 on "Faith and Learning." At that time, we generally agreed there was a great need for literature that could help Christians integrate their Christian faith with the science that was such a powerful and an increasingly influential cultural force.

Sometime later, as I was expressing this sentiment to Cecil Paul, newly appointed president of Eastern Nazarene College, where I teach, he suggested that I might try to "develop a manuscript," which I presumed was publishing jargon for "write a book." The confidence he showed turned out to be just the motivation I needed, and so I began the laborious process of developing a manuscript, which he then read in its entirety, making numerous helpful comments. In the summer of 1992, while this manuscript was being worked on by the publishers, Cecil Paul died tragically and unexpectedly, and I lost my chance to present him with the first copy to come off the presses.

Early in the project, President Paul connected me with an editor at Nazarene Headquarters, a charming fountain of encouragement named Bonnie Perry, who took a hopeful author by the hand and led him through the long process of developing a manuscript exactly twice as long as she originally had suggested would be appropriate.

My colleague, former college roommate, and philosophical brother-in-arms, Paul Nyce, read each chapter of the developing manuscript as it whined off the printer, laboriously filling the margins of the first draft with comments, not all of which were suitable for incorporation into the second draft. "Does it sound like a book?" I asked repeatedly, and he always answered, "Yes."

I must also thank Lowell Hall, who, in spite of having elected to be a chemist rather than a physicist, has proven to be a trusted and valued mentor, friend, and critic. He read the entire manuscript and made numerous suggestions, most of which I sensibly adopted. He also uncovered a few obscure literary misdemeanors, which I was able to eliminate.

My valued colleague, Kathy Frederick of the ENC biology department, read the entire manuscript and, in exchange for a plate of egg rolls and fried rice, made many valuable suggestions. She also verified that my discussion of matters biological wasn't too confused.

Don Christensen, my Sunday School teacher, good friend, frankest critic, and world's smartest layman, read the entire manuscript and convinced me to rewrite chapter 3, which he said was a mess. He was right, of course, and chapter 3 is now much stronger.

A word of appreciation must also be extended to my long-suffering colleagues in the religion department at ENC—Tom Haverly, Henry Spaulding, Laurie Braaten, and Steve McCormick—who put up with, and generally tried to answer, my many questions about their respective fields—I'm sorry my mind seems at times to be somewhat impervious to your particular brand of enlightenment.

I must extend my thanks to those valued colleagues and associates who took the time to read the final draft and responded so positively in writing: Mike McConnell, Al Truesdale, Reuben Welch, Bill McCumber, Max Reams, Sam Jean, Jeff Scheler, and Howard Van Till.

A very special thanks must go to H. Ray Dunning, professor of theology at Trevecca Nazarene College, who carefully read the entire manuscript as it developed, watching closely for the not-so-occasional philosophical and theological faux pas. At his prodding I spent many an evening with my philosophy texts clarifying portions of the manuscript that had flowed too quickly onto the page. There are sections of the final draft where his contributions can be compared only to that of a coauthor. For the countless hours he committed to this project—and his tireless theological tutelage—I will be eternally grateful. (And I will never again caricature Augustine so naively as I did in my original draft!)

Nevertheless, as they always say, the errors that remain are mine and mine alone. An army of advisers can do only so much.

To my preschool daughters, for whom the writing of this book meant less bedtime reading of their far-more-important books, thank you for bearing with me. I will be glad when you learn to read.

And to my wife, Myrna, who gave up the use of our home computer for almost a year, thank you for your encouragement and support.

And finally, and most important, thanks to the Creator for a most interesting world and a most curious mind.

1

Our Worlds and Our Worldviews

• • • • •

The wise man regulates his conduct by the theories both of religion and science.

J. B. S. Haldane (biologist)

• • • • •

Prologue: When Worlds Collide

The coffin stood alone at the front of the church. The church was empty, save for a stricken father who stared in disbelief at the expressionless face of his firstborn son as he slept peacefully on the satin sheets. The father waited for the eyelids to flicker, the mouth to move, the chest to rise and fall; he waited for the child to sit up and announce that he felt much better and would like Daddy to get him a glass of milk.

But Daddy knew that this was not going to happen. His son had been taken from him—the doctors would later determine that diabetes had dealt the fatal blow. And Daddy would spend the rest of his life knowing that his child had died from an illness that modern science had conquered. His precious firstborn had succumbed to a foe that millions were able to control with moderate doses of medication. But his son had not taken the antidote provided by modern science, because his family believed that illnesses were not real. His family believed their religious faith was the appropriate defense against sickness. And this belief had robbed them of a precious life.

They would spend the next few years remembering this day and the events that led up to it. They would remember the

19

stream of medical experts that passed through their lives and told them that their son would die if they did not treat his diabetes—medical experts whose authority they had chosen to ignore. They would remember the long nights spent in prayer as they asked God to please give their son the faith he needed to overcome this evil. They would remember the discussions with their religious leaders, who told them their son would return to health as soon as their faith was adequate—religious experts whose authority they had chosen to follow. And they would learn to grieve that they had listened to the wrong authority.

This is a true story, dramatized in a recent television special. The family in question were members of a religious faith that taught that there is no such thing as sickness—that all sickness is illusory, an evil that moves into a space where faith in God was supposed to reside. Sickness was a problem to be solved by the theologian, not the medical doctor.

This unfortunate incident is a tragic illustration of the confrontation between authorities—in this case the respective authorities of modern science and the doctrines of a particular religious group. Modern science claims to be the authority in matters of health; but, for members of the family described above, their religious doctrine was the authority. Two voices were heard calling out in disagreement, but only one could be heeded.

Science and religion are two powerful voices of authority in our contemporary world, each earning our trust as we learn to appreciate the illumination they shed on the complexity of our experience. Each has a window through which its truth can be observed. Each provides a security of needed explanations for the important questions of our existence. And generally we can hear them both without the confusion felt by the family described above, for the questions of science are not usually the questions of religion.

But science and religion can be made to quarrel if their roles are confused and one attempts to usurp the authority that rightfully belongs to the other. Discord can replace the harmony that should characterize these two authorities.

This book will demonstrate that modern science and the Christian faith, properly understood, should never be in genuine conflict—that all apparent conflicts are either (1) manufactured by overly combative participants with personal agendas or (2) based on a misunderstanding of what science and religion are trying to say with their pronouncements about the world. While there are some religious perspectives, Christian and otherwise, that attempt to usurp the authority of science, this book will argue that when the Christian faith is properly understood, there should be nothing but harmony with science. By the same token, those scientific perspectives that attempt to enlarge themselves into full-blown religious worldviews represent an unwarranted extension of the reasonable domain of science.

The Development of a Worldview

As a first step in understanding the conflict between science and religion it is helpful to examine the origins of our belief system, which we will understand to be the collection of everything we believe and value, both directly and indirectly. This chapter will show that our belief system is not a simple description of reality, both spiritual and physical, that has been handed to us like some comprehensive encyclopedia that contains everything we need to know. Rather, we will see that our belief system, which we will call a worldview, is constructed from a wide variety of sources over the course of many years. In fact, a worldview is intrinsically dynamic, since we really never stop incorporating new information into our concept of reality.

Building a Worldview

Human experience is a complex phenomenon. Our first steps on this long road are taken in a world that is very unfamiliar to us and sometimes even hostile to our fragile presence. The few constants in the chaos become precious to us—parents, a sibling, a crib, a stuffed animal. Their constancy provides security, a shelter from the storm, and we begin to develop a concept of this strange new world.

As our concept grows, the world seems less strange; the randomness becomes regular, the frightening becomes comfortable, the remarkable becomes ordinary. Our world has begun to make sense to us. As we grow older we continue to organize our experiences, always attempting to make sense out of what could seem like vast confusion. We are developing a worldview.

A worldview is an organized scheme that we use to interpret our experiences. It is a system of explanations that provide answers to the questions posed by experience, both directly and indirectly. In *The Universe Next Door*, James Sire suggests that "a world view is a set of presuppositions (assumptions which may be true, partially true or entirely false) which we hold (consciously or unconsciously, consistently or inconsistently) about the basic make-up of our world."[1]

The makeup of our world includes (1) the empirical, or observable, world (What is the basic *stuff* out of which things are made, and how does that stuff change?); (2) the world of values (What things are to be valued, and how will I make value decisions?); and (3) the spiritual world (What is spiritual truth, and how does it relate to me?). At some level, everything we believe to be true is a part of our worldview. In fact, the very criterion by which we decide what is true is a part of this scheme of explanation.

A worldview is necessary to function effectively; without a worldview, our experiences lose their constancy, events lose their interconnectedness, the familiar loses its intimacy. All explanation is lost without a worldview. And we, too, are lost, strangers in a strange land.

Early Beginnings

Newborn infants certainly do not have a meaningful comprehension of anything. They have certain reflexes, one of which will provide nourishment with a little effort. They know how to cry; they have a mysterious, innate comprehension of what a human being looks like; they have what can only be called unrealized potential. More information is needed to begin the process of making sense out of the world. Gradually an organized world emerges from the chaos, however, as patterns are discovered. And these patterns provide an important source of comfort to the developing child.

---

1. James Sire, *The Universe Next Door* (Downers Grove, Ill.: InterVarsity Press, 1988), 17.

As the complexity of the world becomes apparent, our ability to organize it is first strained and then surpassed. "Where did I come from?" I asked as a child, posing a philosophical question whose answer was far beyond the comprehension of my years. My mother responded, "Your father and I have always believed that God gave you to us." Not quite satisfied with this answer, I followed with, "Did He hold me by my hands and lower me down out of heaven?"

We ask our mothers these deep questions because they are our authorities. "Where did I come from?" we ask—because we sense that everything comes from somewhere. And usually the explanation need not expand our world very much to be acceptable: you came from God; you came from the hospital; the stork brought you. Our world is now a little bigger—it has a hospital, a stork, a nursery in the sky. And our worldview has become just a bit more sophisticated. Self-awareness has grown to the point at which we now know that we are a part of this big new world and need an explanation just like everything else.

As we grow older, this big new world loses much of its initial mystery. We discover that we can understand it; we learn how to build concepts from our experiences—concepts that will help us interpret even more of our experiences—and so on. We become confident that we have mastered the challenge of living in the world because we have figured it out. But the price for each answer is an even more difficult question. When the fog shrouding the small mountain has lifted, a much larger fog shrouding a much larger mountain is revealed.

A Worldview Is Dynamic

Figuring out the world—building a worldview—is a *dynamic* process. We are constantly assembling and reassembling the pieces from all those authorities we find ourselves trusting. These pieces fit together to make a picture; this picture is our personal conception of reality—our worldview.

This worldview changes as we change. Once upon a time we lived in a world with a Santa Claus, an Easter Bunny, and a Daddy who could do anything. Those happy citizens of the world of early childhood were born of the innocence that is the birthright of children—the privilege of living for a few precious years in a fantasy world. Eventually, however, reality strolls in and nonchalantly tramples this fantasy world underfoot. Santa Claus must bow and exit.

For most of us, Santa Claus fades from our worldview as comfortably as the blue from our jeans. We are content to let Santa go, led away happily by the hand of common sense. But sometimes Santa Claus isn't willing to go. Sometimes it seems he must first gather our childhood innocence into his tattered empty sack, climb into a tarnished sleigh, and then ride out of our lives, carrying with him some of the confidence we had worked so hard to generate.

Dealing with a changing worldview is challenging. Sometimes the changes occur naturally and the new worldview arises comfortably out of the old, maturing like a beloved grandparent. Sometimes, however, the new worldview won't crystallize without what seems like a total destruction of the old one. And we must walk for a time through an intellectual no-man's-land searching for a resolution of the doubts and questions that led us to discard our former understanding of reality.

As we increase in "wisdom and stature," our understanding of reality changes. My preschool daughters look out at a world that is much different from mine. They don't know that a pregnant woman was just shot in the head by her husband as they emerged from a childbirth class. They don't know what a crack house is or that there is an AIDS epidemic. They don't know that their daddy stands over them every night and prays that the world they are inheriting will be one in which they will feel safe. They don't know that their primitive faith in God will soon be challenged by a secular society. And they don't know that they will find themselves discarding and modifying some of their beliefs as their faith matures.

A Worldview Is Synthetic

Building a worldview is a *synthetic* process. We must simultaneously incorporate insights from many different sources, as an artist mixes paint on a palette. Understanding what these sources are and how they influence our thinking is important in dealing with intellectual conflicts. These sources are too numerous to catalog completely, but we will briefly outline some of the more important ones—experience, family, society, culture, the church, the Scriptures—and then see how these sources interact to give us our view of reality.

Experience. A primary source for our worldview is personal experience. For most people it is the ultimate authority. It is a rare individual for whom experience does not speak loudly and clearly about the world. Experience is our first teacher. As very young children, we find it is all we have. Our first simple concepts are drawn entirely from a set of very limited experiences, over which we have virtually no control.

Successful parenting requires that these initial experiences be provided with careful consideration for the effects that they will have on the child just entering into this complex world. Some of the conclusions we draw during these formative years stay with us all of our lives. Child psychologists[2] suggest that our view of the world as fundamentally friendly or hostile depends in large part on the circumstances of our first year of life—circumstances over which children have virtually no control.

Experience remains the primary authority in our lives, never playing second fiddle to the other authorities in our intellectual orchestra. "Seeing is believing" always rings true, if we can generalize *seeing* to include the perceptions of any of our senses. Even though Thomas doubted that Jesus could have risen from the dead, he became fully convinced when he observed his risen Lord. The experience of seeing Christ communicated with far more authority than intellectual arguments about the impossibility of people rising from the dead.

As a physicist, I happen to believe that it is impossible for creatures from an alien world to visit the earth. Conventional physics can provide a number of very convincing proofs that the distance is too great, the time too long, and so on. Virtually all physicists share my conviction that, when people claim to have interacted with aliens, they are either deluded or lying. But this belief, currently sitting securely on an impregnable scientific foundation, would become a house of cards to be easily collapsed by a single identifiable alien if it should walk into the

---

2. See, for example, Burton White, *The First Three Years of Life* (New York: Avon, 1975).

room, raise a three-fingered hand in greeting, and say whatever it is that aliens say.

It is generally true that we are most comfortable with that portion of our worldview that derives directly from our own experiences. Being convinced of a fact through some form of argumentation is far less meaningful than experiencing that fact directly.

We trust our experiences. They are the first and most powerful elements in our worldview.

Family. Family is another important source of information about our world. As children, our initial questions are all directed at our parents, who must then frame answers within the narrow confines of our limited experience. These answers are then weighed in our primitive intellectual balances and accepted or rejected. Rejection means that the explanation did not fit into the existing worldview, simple as it may be. My three-year-old daughter, for example, does not believe that water from the faucet is the same as water from the jug in the refrigerator (the jug was filled from the faucet). Her parents' explanations do not fit just yet.

Family may teach us about the value of cooperation. If we learned that the rights of others are as important as our rights, then we probably learned it from our family. If we learned to respect the wisdom of experience, it is because a parent or another adult model demonstrated that wisdom.

Once this second source of authority becomes recognized as a legitimate source for information about the world, the potential for conflict emerges. This authority outside ourselves, not based on our own experience, may suggest that certain of the ideas we have developed on our own are not correct. My daughter, for example, has a well-developed sense of what, when, and where it is appropriate to eat; her concept of eating candy at night in her bed is, however, at odds with other, more traditional culinary concepts suggested by the other authority in her life: her parents. Already the conflict between authorities emerges.

Appropriately realized, the family is an effective force in a child's intellectual development. For many of us, it is a source of information and perspectives on the world that never loses its strength.

Society. As soon as we develop peer relationships, we find ourselves listening to yet another authority. We may discover that the approval of peers is very important to us; to get this approval we may be willing to set aside some of the things in which we have placed our trust. In the best of all worlds, society reinforces the values we have acquired through experience and from our family. In the real world, however, society challenges our fragile value system. Adolescent rebellion, for example, erupts when children begin to disconnect themselves from the intellectual umbilical cord that has fed and nourished their developing worldview.

There are powerful messages that we receive from our social interactions. Some are healthy; some are not. One of the unfortunate communications that emerges all too frequently from society is prejudice—racial, sexual, economic, religious, intellectual. It is a rare individual who doesn't at least hear this message somewhere along the way. In a variety of subtle ways, society informs each group that it is the *chosen*—chosen because of its race, economic level, religion, intelligence—and the rest are the outsiders.

In subtle ways that seem almost beyond our control, we find ourselves listening to the voice of our society. And sometimes we trust it.

Culture. Contemporary culture exerts a powerful influence on our worldview, although sometimes in ways that may not seem very important. If we look within ourselves objectively, we will discover the many ways our culture has shaped our views of reality. This inward look may reveal a predisposition toward European cars, suntans, designer clothes, and Oriental cuisine—all things that were far less important or even irrelevant to previous generations. We may discover that we like popular music better than classical music; we may be dismayed at our preference for television over great literature. These preferences reflect the many ways our culture subtly communicates its perspectives and values to us.

We discover that we are citizens of a larger world and that we have a need to feel comfortable in this larger world. Subtly, we begin to acquire values from our culture.

Our culture may communicate to us that greatness is obtained by selflessly contributing to the welfare of others. Mother Teresa is certainly one of the great citizens of our century and has been appropriately recognized as such. On the other hand, self-promoting rock stars generally receive far more praise—and certainly far more money!—than Mother Teresa. With some vagueness about the meaning of *great*, our society considers these rock stars to be greater than Mother Teresa.

To the extent that we share the values and priorities of our culture—and we all do to some degree—it is because we have subtly learned to trust the messages our culture is sending. We read the billboards, we shop from the catalogs, we watch the television programs—and we hear the message.

Scripture. For many of us, the Scriptures are an important contributor to our worldview. As children, we learned the Bible stories even as we learned to talk. The first songs we learned to sing were about simple Bible concepts and stories. We learned to put a great deal of trust in the person who stands behind the pulpit and reads the Bible on Sunday morning. Our familiarity with the Bible and respect for it grow until it becomes a significant force in our lives. We may even become uncomfortable setting objects on top of our Bibles, as if the physical book itself was somehow an object of reverence.

The Scriptures inform us about the issues in life that seem the most important. We discover that our legal system grew from a seed that was planted on Mount Sinai. The teachings of Jesus Christ inspire us in ways beyond our comprehension. The Scriptures seem somehow to guide us into the presence of God.

The Bible does not announce its truths to us directly, however; it must be read, interpreted, and understood before its message can be received. Thus the Bible does not possess the clarity of personal experience. Those of us without training in biblical languages must read a translation whose message is slightly colored by the translator's choice of words; furthermore, the meanings associated with the words themselves change with each generation and must be interpreted anew in light of these changes. This interpretation is sometimes personal, but more often the Scriptures are interpreted through the traditions of the church, traditions that most of us find ourselves trusting implicitly.

The Christian Tradition. The Christian tradition is the collective wisdom of the Church as it has received, understood, and communicated the message of the gospel from the first century. Many of the things we consider straightforward in the Bible only seem that way because the Church has developed a tradition of interpretation that has been handed down to us. For example, we have a Bible that has a certain number of books in it, 27 in the New Testament and 39 in the Old Testament. We refer to this select group as the Canon of Scripture. For several centuries the Canon had no such clear description; eventually, however, the Canon became established through traditional usage, and the Bible assumed its present form.

Many of the specific doctrines that come readily to mind when we read the Bible are the result of historical traditions that find their origin in the writings of influential church leaders. Creation is ex nihilo (out of nothing), because early theologians needed to combat a heresy about matter, and thus our bodies, being evil. Original sin was associated with sex for several centuries, because a fourth-century bishop named Augustine found that connection to be personally relevant and assumed that what was true for him was true in general. The sinful nature of man thus became hereditary, to be passed on to successive generations like red hair or blue eyes. The Catholic tradition developed the doctrine of the Immaculate Conception of Mary as a necessary antecedent to the birth of Jesus without a sinful nature. Even today, this notion still colors our thinking about sin. Sexual sin is widely considered to be far more serious than *ordinary* sins like lying, cheating, and so on.

For those in the Calvinist tradition, the Scriptures speak loudly about the sovereignty of God and softly about the will of man. For Arminians, the reverse is true. Wesleyans read the Bible carefully and find two works of grace, while Baptists read those same Scriptures and find just one. What we discover in the Scriptures depends strongly, but almost invisibly, on our religious tradition.

Many contemporary religious scholars recognize that there is a certain collective wisdom in the traditions of the Church and that they should be considered as sources of authority. Theologians who operate on the cutting edge of their discipline without due consideration of their tradition soon find themselves falling over that edge. But, alas, the various traditions disagree with each other—which makes at least some of them wrong.

A very simple example of a common tradition is that of the three wise men. The Scriptures, surprisingly, make no reference to *three* men at all—three gifts, perhaps, but an unnumbered group of wise men from the East. The popularity of this notion is reflected in the millions of cards sent each year with three wise men on them; Nativity scenes across the country with three wise men; songs like "We Three Kings," etc. If it seems impossible to the reader that there could have been any other number of wise men than three, then tradition has done a good job of shaping the mental images you associate with Christmas. For most of us, it is hard even to read the Christmas story in the New Testament without picturing three wise men.

Just as our culture helps shape the secular part of our worldview by putting collective interpretations on our experiences, so the Christian tradition shapes the theological part of our worldview by imposing interpretations on the Scriptures and our religious experience.

Science. The final contributor to our worldview that we will discuss in this short survey is science. Science has achieved a status in the modern world that is unparalleled in history. Of all the authorities in our modern world, it is the one that seems most comfortable challenging the others; it is the one that aggressively asserts its conclusions, seemingly without fear of contradiction. It is the one that greedily eyes the domains of the others and tries to explain away their phenomena.

The Status of Science

The confidence with which science makes its pronouncements about the world has been generated during the past three centuries as science has achieved considerable success in discovering useful information about the world. The utility of science has been demonstrated in the ways it has improved our lives. Great plagues no longer sweep across continents wiping out large fractions of population. The current AIDS epidemic cannot even be compared to the great plagues that ravaged Europe in past centuries. The Black Plague, for example, killed 4 out of 10 Europeans in the 14th century, and yet that disease has now been completely subdued by advances in medicine. Science has put people on the moon, extracted energy from the nucleus of the atom, and charted the rate at which the continents are drifting apart. Science has built great weapons that can literally blow our planet into small pieces—certainly an impressive accomplishment, though it has left the world somewhat nervous. Science can predict the exact second of the next eclipse and measure the time it takes to reflect a laser beam from the earth to the moon and back.

We all pay some homage to science every day—the food we eat, the cars we drive, the computers we use, the medicines we take, the devices by which we communicate—and we all recognize that science[3] has certainly made impressive contributions to our modern society, not all of which are deserving of praise.

Science is indeed a powerful voice of authority and one that is effective in communicating its wisdom to our society. Its strength is derived from its success; science could not have performed all of its magic unless it somehow knew something about the world. Those who would criticize and even dismiss the significance of science because of its tendency to constantly change its mind need only consider the impact of science on their lives to realize the folly of this position. The proof of science is in its pudding.

---

3. Technically speaking, most of our interaction with "science" is through the offspring of science—technology. The fact that nuclear (or chemical) weapons exist today reflects a *political* commitment on the part of governments to develop the *technology* to produce such devices. The production of weapons (or synthetic clothing for that matter) is only of minor *scientific* interest. Once the fundamental theories have been developed to describe a phenomenon or process, science loses interest and technology takes over. Science lives in the world of ideas; technology lives in the world of machines and products. For our purposes in this discussion and much of what follows, we will consider science to include technology, which is the way it is generally perceived by the nonspecialist.

So we listen to science as it tells us things about this world in which we live, even though those things don't agree with our immediate experience. The earth, for example, is not flat—even though it certainly looks that way from our windows. The earth is rushing around the sun at over 60,000 miles per hour, even though we can't feel it. The continents are drifting. Space is warped. Our sun is 93 million miles away. Space has black holes in it. The world is made of small particles that no one can see. Matter can be turned into energy. Genes from our parents determine what we look like. And so on. Our society pays intellectual allegiance to all of these *crazy* ideas, because we are uncomfortable challenging the conclusions of science. Our worldview informs us that the voice of science is one to which we should listen.

It is remarkable that we accept all of this. We have not experienced any of it directly. Unless we are scientists ourselves, we really cannot produce a strong argument for any of these assertions. We accept all of these unbelievable claims solely on the basis of the authority of science. We believe science understands the universe even when its explanation runs counter to our common sense.

In fact, we are more than willing to go beyond mere intellectual assent; we will even place our very lives on the scientific altar in hospitals every day. We pay doctors to stick needles into our arms and introduce mysterious chemicals into our blood because they tell us it is a good idea. We let them cut us open and take out parts of our bodies and replace them with ones made of plastic and stainless steel. We charge them with the responsibility of keeping us alive when our bodies have mechanical failures.

Furthermore, on those occasions in the past when science has been challenged, it has triumphed. No conclusion legitimately drawn by science has ever been successfully assailed by another authority. When Adolf Hitler's political convictions led him to reject the results of Jewish physics, Germany lost her position of scientific leadership and was unable to build an atomic bomb. When Marxists in Russia insisted, on the basis of their ideology, that it was the environment and not the genes that controlled the development of an animal, Soviet biology went into a tailspin from which it is just now emerging. And, as we shall consider in more detail later, when Galileo's critics advanced arguments based on theology that the earth could not be moving around the sun, they found themselves flailing with a feeble and inappropriate weapon against an unexpectedly resilient enemy.

These examples should not be used to argue that everyone believes, or even should believe, all that science claims as truth. Rather, the claim is that science seems to be the final authority in those matters on which it is qualified to comment. But this remarkable competence, which is strictly limited to the description and control of the natural world, has led some to diminish the value of those authorities that address questions in other areas, questions that do not have the neat and tidy answers characteristic of science.

A Worldview Is Individual

Daniel Taylor wrote, "Every person, whether reflective or not, has a way of making sense out of the world. It is as fundamental a need as eating and breathing. We have a compulsion for ordering and explaining our experiences, even if we decide that the governing principle of life is disorder."[4]

All of us construct our own individual view of reality. At a very detailed level, a person's worldview is as unique as his or her fingerprints. From a broader perspective, however, members of a given cultural-religious group will have very similar perspectives. In fact, one of the strongest sources of identity for a group is their shared worldview. The Amish communities are characterized by an extremely homogeneous worldview that is radically different from that of the larger culture in which they generally reside. Members of fringe religious sects like the Hare Krishnas and the Moonies also have distinctive worldviews, much to the chagrin of *normal* people who don't like to be pestered by people selling flowers in airports.

The worldviews each of us possesses have been constructed from a variety of sources, all of which have some claim to

---

4. Daniel Taylor, *The Myth of Certainty* (Waco, Tex.: Word Publishers, 1986), 21.

authority. If they had no claim to authority, then we would not trust them. For most of us, some of these sources have an ultimate authority that is not to be challenged. There are skeptics who will place their confidence only in their personal experience, refusing to trust authorities outside themselves. There are scientists who will trust only the computer printouts emerging from their experimental apparatus. There are religious fundamentalists who will trust only their traditional interpretations of the Bible. And there are playboys who will listen only to the empty voice of their culture.

There are, however, no single-source worldviews. And where there is more than one source of authority there can be disagreement, especially if the domain of each is not appropriately respected.

Worldviews in Flux

All of the sources mentioned earlier, and others as well, inform us to varying degrees about the nature of this world in which we live. With different levels of confidence, we consider each of these sources to have some authority in some area. But there is no established procedure to identify the correct authority to answer a particular question. It seems the family in the story at the beginning of this chapter listened to the wrong authority. But that was not clear to them at the time, and they paid a terrible price for the information.

As our dynamic worldview attempts to incorporate new ideas into its larger structure, internal strains are placed on the worldview. The simple explanations that grow out of apparently simple experience must be discarded when the full complexity of that experience becomes evident. But new ideas can be incorporated into an existing worldview without conflict only when these new ideas are compatible with the explanatory scheme already in place.

Most of the ideas children get from parents expand the existing conceptual framework rather than modify it. It is always easier to bring new ideas on board when they do not require us to make room for them by throwing old ideas overboard. Psychologists refer to this as the preference for accommodation over assimilation.

In grade school, most of what we learn is new—and so not in conflict with previously held notions. We accommodate the new ideas. Even scientific discoveries, to the extent that we are aware of them, rarely require that we rethink our view of reality and can thus be easily accommodated. We tend to find the truths of our religious commitments comfortably constant as our spiritual awareness matures. And as we grow up, the messages from our peers lose their importance as we internalize our values. For most of us, the development of our adult worldview is a straightforward accumulation of many little bits of wisdom, all of which seem to fit comfortably together into the big picture.

But occasionally a piece of the new picture just won't fit into any of the holes in the old picture. Sometimes it is necessary to make room for new insights by discarding old ideas. The world of the adult is much more complicated than the world of the child and demands a much different sort of explanation.

In this book we will be discussing some of the problems that have emerged as the human race has grown up and primitive ways of looking at the world have had to be replaced with more sophisticated ones. In each historical epoch there have been new ideas struggling for the hearts and minds of those people who most clearly saw that the old explanations had outlived their usefulness. But people are reluctant to change their worldviews, so grand arguments erupted over such details as the roundness, motion, and age of the earth; the equality of the races; the intelligence of women; the origin of the human race; and so on.

Epilogue

This chapter opened with a story about a family who inadvertently allowed their child to die because they were not comfortable placing the authority of the medical community above that of their religious faith. Within their worldview, the problem of sickness was not medical—it was spiritual. Their tragedy occurred because they chose the wrong authority to solve the problem of sickness.

All worldviews have internal conflicts. The appropriate resolution of such conflicts requires an identification of the authority that should prevail within the context of that conflict.

Sometimes it is as easy to find the authority to resolve a conflict in a worldview as it is to find a doctor when you are sick. But it is essential to recognize that no single authority can answer all questions. Religious questions like the meaning of grace cannot be answered by science. Cultural issues like who should be *Time* magazine's "Person of the Year" cannot be resolved by reference to the Bible. Just as we do not ask plumbers to fix problems with our teeth, we must not turn to the wrong authority to answer specific questions within our worldview.

"Whatever the world view, it must deal with opposition. No belief system is comfortable with competing systems, not even those which claim to be. At the deepest level difference threatens. It challenges our sense of security."[5]

The Conflict Between Science and Religion

Our society (Western civilization) is distinguished from the rest of the world primarily by its (1) science and its (2) religion, which is Christianity in its various manifestations. After a stormy introduction 500 years ago at the beginning of the Renaissance, these two important authorities began the long, uneasy conversation that can still be heard in courtrooms across the nation as legislators haggle over the issue of creation and evolution.

The battle lines in this war are hard to locate, and it is frequently difficult to tell which side is which. On one side of the courtroom, theologians contend that evolution is science and scientists assert that evolution is religion. On the other side of the courtroom, different scientists and different theologians argue the opposite.

The issue boils down to one of *authority*. Who should decide what is true in questions relating to origins? Is the origin and development of the human race a scientific or a theological question? Is the correct explanation for the origin of the universe to be found in the astronomy textbook or the Bible? Or can the Bible and the textbook *both* address this question in complementary ways?

---

5. Ibid., 24.

For most of the Christian era it has been the church that dominated such discussions.

Over the course of the past couple of centuries, however, science has gradually acquired the upper hand and can now even be heard to claim complete authority. Along the way, both sides were constantly challenging each other as they attempted to find the line that separated their respective domains. Unfortunately, this line is fuzzy, and disagreement still remains about exactly where it is located. Thus we find ourselves confronted with a call to arms and insistence that we must beat our ploughshares into swords in order to wage an unholy war with the enemy..It is one of the tragedies of our time that science and religion find themselves at war.

In the next chapter we will consider the positions of both scientific and religious extremists as they display their hostility toward each other. We will see that this conflict is historical in nature and, like an old family feud, is something the present generation should put to rest.

2

The Unholy War

• • • • •

The Bible teaches us how to go to heaven,
Not how the heavens go.

Galileo Galilei

• • • • •

In the previous chapter we noted that it is possible for religion and science to engage in swordplay. This occurs when either transgresses the boundaries of its proper domain and invades the realm properly belonging to the other. When, for example, scientists investigate religious phenomena with the same approach they would use in the investigation of natural phenomena, the result is usually an attempt to explain away religion, rather than understand it on its own terms.

In the same way, when theologians argue on religious grounds that the natural world must be constructed in a certain way or have originated by a certain process, the result is usually an attempt to explain away the theories of science. This attempt by science and religion to explain away the phenomena of the other is an unholy war—an unnecessary and divisive quarrel based on a misunderstanding of the nature of the respective disciplines.

This misunderstanding starts with the failure to recognize the nature and limits of (1) the methods appropriate to each field and (2) the nature of the phenomena investigated by each field. The unholy war is declared when the methods and the phenomena of one field are presumed to lie within the province of the other.

The successes of science, as we observed in the previous chapter, have caused some scientists to violate this separation by seeking to interpret the whole of reality according to the criteria of the scientific method. One such example of this is scientific materialism. This is a worldview based on the belief that everything—absolutely everything—should be explicable in terms of scientific concepts. Starting with this restrictive assumption, scientific materialism can provide only rather incredible explanations for such phenomena as a mother's love for her baby. The following account is based on Richard Dawkins' popular science book, *The Selfish Gene*, which is written from the perspective of scientific materialism.

The One Who Dies with the Most Children Wins

Buried deep within the human body is a remarkable blueprint known as the genetic code. This blueprint contains all the information necessary to construct a human being—the eye color, the skin tone, the hair, the height, the tendency toward obesity, and so on. This genetic blueprint consists of 46 chromosomes, half of which came from an egg supplied by the mother. The other half came from one of the half billion sperm provided by the father. The genetic code originates when the egg is fertilized by the single successful sperm that manages to make it to the egg ahead of the rest of the unfortunate pack. This lucky sperm is the one that fate has chosen to perform the essential task of reproduction. The other sperm all die, having lived in vain, their meager existence squandered in Mother Nature's ultimate game of chance.

When this extraordinary event transpires, a complete genetic code is established, one that has the potential to build a most remarkable machine. If all goes well, the newly fertilized egg will now embark on a truly miraculous journey. One day after fertilization the cell will split in two, then four, then eight, as it repeatedly divides, making copies of itself. Then it begins the mysterious process of differentiation in which division moves beyond mere copying into the production of different specialized cells.

The number of cells in the developing embryo numbers in the thousands, then the millions, then the billions and beyond as the organism begins to develop. Bumps appear around the edges of what looks like a formless blob; those bumps extend to become arms and legs. Smaller bumps turn into fingers and toes, clearly visible within six weeks of conception.

A functioning heart, liver, kidneys, and lungs form as the genetic code supervises the construction of the machine. Potentiality becomes actuality. An extraordinary computer develops, protected with the comfortable confines of an almost impregnable housing in the head of the organism. Detectors capable of responding to sounds, sights, smells, touches, and tastes accompany that computer.

About nine months after fertilization, when the time is right, a mysterious signal announces that the organism is ready to be born, to be physically separated from the body of the mother that has protected it since it began.

Something called a "baby" emerges, utterly helpless, into a hostile world, but that is not usually a problem. The genetic code of the "mother" has already programmed her to focus an extraordinary amount of attention on the new baby because, instinctively, she knows that the genetic code of the baby is really a copy of her genetic code. She must guarantee the survival of the new arrival, for it is an extension of herself, of her genetic blueprint. What she thinks is love for her child is nothing but an all-consuming obsession to extend her genes one more generation in the future.

Meanwhile the genetic code of the baby guides its development through infancy, puberty, adolescence, and into adulthood. At the onset of adulthood the organism will suddenly find itself obsessed with the need to reproduce. Hormones programmed by the genetic blueprint are released. An overwhelming need to make more copies of its genetic code becomes a consuming passion. Only personal and social restraint will prevent it from making innumerable copies of itself.

The adult organism is driven with the most powerful of motivations to make additional copies of its genetic code so that the code will survive even after the human being has ceased to exist. The machine whose development was directed by the genetic code was created solely for the purpose of making copies of itself. The production of these copies is the ultimate purpose of its existence.

The machine that dies with the most copies of itself is the winner.

This is the "Selfish Gene"—the program written within the egg upon fertilization. This gene is selfish because it insists that reproducing itself is the most important thing in the universe. This gene has evolved a strong body to surround it, protect it from the elements, and ensure its survival; this gene has developed a powerful brain to coordinate the functions relevant to its survival; this gene has developed a system of hormones that drive its host to reproduce. This gene has so organized its host that it cannot help but survive and reproduce.

The purpose for the human race is the survival and reproduction of the genetic codes that lie within us. The bodies and brains associated with these codes are secondary. Art, music, religion, even happiness are all irrelevant except as they contribute to this fundamental purpose. The real show on planet earth is the competition among the peculiar molecules called genes as they continue the eternal struggle for survival that began hundreds of millions of years ago, in the seas of a primordial earth when they were known as replicators. The replicators that used to live in the sea found that living in people had more survival value. So they evolved human beings to be their guardians—their survival machines.

> Now they swarm in huge colonies, safe inside gigantic lumbering robots, sealed off from the outside world, communicating with it by tortuous indirect routes, manipulating it by remote control. They are in you and in me; they created us, body and mind; and their preservation is the ultimate rationale for our existence. They have come a long way, those replicators. Now they go by the name of genes, and we are their survival machines.[1]

* * *

This frightening and demoralizing perspective is the basis for the worldview of Richard Dawkins, the author of *The Selfish*

---

1. Richard Dawkins, *The Selfish Gene* (New York: Oxford University Press, 1976), 21.

Gene. It is a stark and barren world, with little to inspire comfort. It describes a planet on which no one would choose to live. But it is inhabited by 5 billion packages of selfish genes, each working to maximize its own chances for survival.

The one who dies with the most children wins.

Outline

In the next part of this chapter we will discuss the worldview of scientific materialism as an example of a completely nonreligious scheme of explanation. This perspective on nature comes by default when religion is ignored as a possible explanation for some of the more profound dimensions of our existence and its territory is invaded by science. We will then consider the potential antagonism that can exist between science and religion as expressed by representatives of the extreme ends of the spectrum. A prominent astronomer will argue that religion is a dangerous delusion; a fundamentalist Christian will counter that science is a dangerous and satanic plot.

In the middle of the chapter we will argue that science and religion have never had a truly normal relationship and that it is not possible to reduce their interaction to some simple formula—a norm that may have existed during some particularly enlightened period of history. One of the primary reasons for this complexity is the irregular way that science entered Western culture. Only after a millennium of undiluted and unchallenged religious authority was science brought into the discussion. By this point the beliefs and attitudes of the Christian Church were extremely well developed and thus were uncomfortable with the challenges provided by the new science.

In the last part of the chapter we will introduce the current stormy relationship between the fundamentalist church and modern science on the issue of human origins. We will argue briefly here and in more detail later that the current argument over creation and evolution is so similar to the argument about the moving earth at the time of Galileo that we would be well advised to learn the lessons of that history in order to avoid repeating its mistakes.

The Worldview of Scientific Materialism

The worldview described in the preamble to this chapter is that of the prominent evolutionary biologist Richard Dawkins. It is called scientific materialism. It is a worldview that recognizes the authority of science only. Science is thus considered competent to explain the purpose of existence, if existence can be said to have a purpose.[2] The extraordinary hypothesis described in Dawkins' *Selfish Gene* argues that human history is nothing but a predetermined contest to see whose genes can reproduce themselves the greatest number of times. Making genetic copies of ourselves is the purpose and meaning of our existence, but purpose and meaning have been reduced to function.

This worldview—scientific materialism—is at the extreme end of the scientific spectrum. When science has pushed aside all other authorities and claimed the entire world for itself, the result is the loss of anything that looks like real meaning in the universe. Art, music, literature, even religion are just the incidental ravings of a species whose purpose is simply to reproduce itself; culture is simply the irrelevant by-product of the remarkable mind that evolved to take care of the genes and figure out how to reproduce them.

How can anyone hold this disturbing perspective? How can such a worldview attract great minds to the feeble flicker of its lonely candle? And if one is somehow attracted to this faint illumination, what motivation is there to write a book about it? Why describe in great detail the inner workings of a meaningless universe? Writing a book, in fact, is a waste of time from the perspective of *The Selfish Gene;* such an enterprise is a distraction from the production of genetic copies.

Scientific materialism is a worldview that can be assembled entirely from the raw material of science, without input from any of the other authorities mentioned in the first chapter. People who find scientific materialism attractive do so because of

---

2. Scientific materialism is the scientific foundation of the broader philosophical movement known as secular humanism. Within the broad outlines of this worldview, many of its adherents claim they can develop adequate quasi-religious definitions for concepts such as purpose, morality, and so on.

its dependence upon science as sole authority. If you perceive that science is the only credible authority available and are drawn to the type of explanations it provides, then you can easily make yourself at home in the house of scientific materialism.

But most people are quite uncomfortable in the house of scientific materialism—and for good reason. Who decided science should be the only authority? Why should the claims of all other authorities be subordinated to that of science? Can we really dismiss all of the vast religious experience of humankind as futile groping in the dark—an incidental by-product of our aggressive genes? Is the selfishness of our genes really adequate to explain everything? Is religious experience invalid just because it is hard to analyze from a scientific point of view?

Scientific materialism, or scientism, is a significant worldview today. Many of the great thinkers of our time subscribe to it. This century has seen the growth of scientism and the decline of the generally accepted theistic worldview that was common in all previous centuries. It can certainly be argued that science has replaced religion as the primary authority for many people today.

But this situation is the climax of a long series of confrontations in which the religious worldview gradually lost ground in the wider culture. Unfortunately, much of religion's loss of credibility has resulted from the church's own failure to recognize its proper domain. When it sanctified certain scientific theories in the name of revelation, it both misunderstood the nature of revelation and set itself up for embarrassing defeats. The church would like to forget that it ever denied the roundness of the earth, the races of people on the other side of the planet, the moons around Jupiter, the existence of comets, the reality of fossils—all because it claimed to have a revelation that told them otherwise.

In the next two chapters we will examine some of the historical shifts that took place in Western society as the almost totally theistic worldview of the medieval Christian Church was at first challenged and then dramatically altered by a series of scientific developments.

Science and Religion: Ploughshares or Swords?

To understand this complicated relationship, it is helpful to consider the difference between science and religion as sources of authority. We use the term *authority* here to refer to the respect acquired through the successful provision of explanations that help order our world and our lives. We tend to trust explanations that make sense to us and, over time, begin to develop a confidence in particularly helpful authorities, just as we are drawn toward people we feel give good advice.

Some modern scholars would like to argue that religion cannot be trusted to give good advice, that there are problems with religion's claim to authority. Some of these problems include the following views: (1) that there are many great world religions, only one of which can be correct. How can the Christian faith claim to be true in any ultimate sense when there seems to be no effective way to challenge an identical claim made by a Muslim or a Buddhist? (2) That religion has historically produced strife and discord as opposing zealots have gone as far as to take up arms against each other. For many people, this has greatly damaged the credibility of religion. Furthermore, even within a relatively homogeneous religious group such as the evangelical Christian Church, there is a discouraging amount of disagreement and name-calling. (3) That there seems to be very little progress in religion in the sense of figuring something out upon which we all can agree. It certainly does not appear that religion is zeroing in on any discernible truth or that the grand efforts of centuries of careful theological reflection have produced any unity. In fact, the opposite seems to be the case, as the Christian Church has divided into East and West, Catholic and Protestant, and then the dividing continues within Protestantism as the various traditions continue to splinter into the plethora of denominations we encounter today.

On the other hand, the claim that science makes to authority has gained in credibility on exactly these same points: (1) that there is only one science and that science transcends cultural, linguistic, and political barriers, making laboratory partners out of political enemies; (2) that historically there has been very little quarreling in the name of science, and great upheavals have generally occurred with no loss of life; (3) that the progress of science is indisputable and a great many issues have been successfully settled and now serve as foundations upon which future generations can comfortably build.[3] Furthermore, science tends to embrace its truths with more humility than religion, always allowing that new theories may improve upon old ones. Religion, on the other hand, generally maintains that it has the truth currently in hand.

For many, these differences suggest that religion is in some way inferior to science. Consider the following criticism of organized religion by physicist Hermann Bondi, one of the premier astronomers of this century.

> Generally the state of mind of a believer in a revelation is the awful arrogance of saying "I *know*, and those who do not agree with my belief are wrong." In no other field is such arrogance so widespread, in no other field do people feel so utterly certain of the "knowledge." It is to me quite disgusting that anybody should feel so superior, so selected and chosen against all the many who differ in their beliefs or unbeliefs. This would be bad enough, but so many believers do their best to propagate their faith, at the very least to their children but often also to others (and historically there are, of course, plenty of examples of doing this by force and ruthless brutality). The fact that stares one in the face is that people of the greatest sincerity and of all levels of intelligence differ and have always differed in their religious beliefs. Since at most one faith can be true, it follows that *human beings are extremely liable to believe firmly and honestly in something untrue in the field of revealed religion.* One would have expected this obvious fact to lead to some humility, to some thought that however deep one's faith, one may conceivably be mistaken. Nothing is further from the believer, any believer, than this elementary humility. All in his

---

3. It should be pointed out that many people are quite concerned with the "dark side" of science. But science *qua science* does not really have a dark side. The problems with nuclear weapons, the environment, the dehumanization of workers, and so on are all the results of the *application* of scientific ideas, which is technology, not science. Technology grows out of decisions made by people to apply knowledge of the natural world to achieve some goal or purpose.

power (which nowadays in a developed country tends to be confined to his children) must have his faith rammed down their throats. In many cases children are indeed indoctrinated with the disgraceful thought that they belong to the one group with superior knowledge who alone have a private wire to the office of the Almighty, all others being less fortunate than they themselves.[4]

This lengthy quote speaks eloquently about the credibility problem some people feel has developed with respect to religious authority. The author is a respected physicist who speaks for many of his colleagues. His criticisms are laden with emotion but are not entirely devoid of truth.

In the other corner of the ring, science is being challenged by certain religious groups who maintain that religion provides all relevant truth and that science cannot be trusted. Representing a viewpoint that seems to have been resurrected from a long-deceased worldview, this perspective claims that all real truth is to be found in the Bible and that science, to the extent that it disagrees with the Bible, cannot be trusted. If science seems to contradict the Bible as they interpret it, then that science is in error and will shortly be corrected by a new and improved science—one that will confirm the biblical position.

Those who support this antiscientific position frequently claim that the motivation for science is *not* the noble and dispassionate pursuit of truth as the scientists so proudly claim but rather the undermining of religious belief. With this hidden agenda as primary motivation, the scientific community, they say, has engaged in a centuries-long conspiracy to promote a collection of lies designed to destroy the credibility of the Bible. Through the tinted glasses of this explanation, the big bang theory, psychoanalysis, and evolution are all promoted by the scientific community, not because they are good explanations for observed phenomenon, but because these are precisely the theories necessary to discredit the biblical revelation. Science is thus seen as a tool of Satan.

---

4. Hermann Bondi, "Religion Is a Good Thing," in *Lying Truths*, ed. R. Duncan and M. Weston-Smith (New York: Pergamon Press, 1979), 205-6. © 1979 by Pergamon Press Ltd. Reprinted with kind permission from Pergamon Press Ltd., Headington Hill Hall, Oxford OX3 0BW, U.K.

This collection of false scientific theories is usually gathered together under the umbrella of secular humanism, the current buzzword for the enemy of the historic Christian faith. Together with the new morality, the new age, the new wave, new music, and all else that might be "new under the sun," the new science is an ally on the wrong side of the battle between the forces of good and evil. Satan is the leader of this new movement, and he has an army of demons coordinating the assault on religion. A typical expression of this view declares:

> Secular humanism has built a wall of reason around the human mind, insulating many from belief in the true God. Now, in the next stage of man's decline, Satan and his demons penetrate the prison of reason, offering a fulfillment which secularism lacks. Always disguising themselves, they blend "spiritual experience" with science, nutrition, the environmental movement, medicine, yoga, hypnotism, and a host of other Eastern teachings. Beginning with small steps, they lead individuals down the path to altered states of consciousness, so that their devilish control can be strengthened.[5]

These competing descriptions and evaluations are, fortunately, caricatures of both religion and science. Only a small minority of scientists share Bondi's low view of the value of religion; in fact many scientists are deeply religious. By the same token, most Christians would disagree that modern science is a tool of Satan, and many are eager to learn about science because of the role it plays in explaining the mysteries of creation. Nevertheless, a real conflict exists as certain very vocal antagonists on both sides issue a call for us to beat our ploughshares into swords in order to wage an unholy war.

Science and Religion: Friends and Foes

The relationship between science and religion is dynamic and multidimensional; it cannot be reduced to some simple formula as many authors with particular agendas have attempted to do. Andrew Dickson White, the first president of Cornell

---

5. Erwin W. Lutzer and John DeVries, *Satan's Evangelistic Strategy for This New Age* (Wheaton, Ill.: Victor Books, 1989), 102.

University, argued that a constant state of warfare is the appropriate description of the interaction of science and religion. He titled his book *A History of the Warfare of Science with Theology in Christendom*. This massive and influential work, which appeared around the turn of the present century, became the starting point for many of the discussions that followed.

At the time White wrote his book, he was president of the first school in the United States with a secular charter, and his university was under harsh criticism from other mainline schools, like Harvard, Yale, and Dartmouth, all of which had religious affiliations. From that unique perspective, perhaps, the relationship between science and theology did look like inevitable warfare. At least, that was how White saw it.

On the other side of the spectrum, some contemporary analysts who desperately want science and theology to be friends are attempting to argue that the warfare White describes was just an illusion. They claim that certain aggressive members of the scientific community in the 19th century felt it would serve the interests of science to portray religion as an enemy. So these polemicists engaged in a smear campaign designed to convince everyone that religion has always been opposed to science (and thus to progress). The conclusion, of course, was that religion should be discredited as a legitimate source of authority.[6]

This book will argue that there is truth on both sides and that balance is required. A truly adequate modern worldview must embrace both science and religion; there need be no intellectual swords crossed in battle. It is not true that science and religion must quarrel, and it is not true that science and religion have been constantly at war. On the other hand, in every era there have been *some* Christians quarreling with *some* scientists about *some* questions of mutual interest.

The broad focus of our argument will be the current controversy over the alleged disagreement between the theories of modern science and the biblical accounts of origins. The reader is no doubt aware of some of the recent highly publicized con-

---

6. Colin A. Russell, "The Conflict Metaphor and Its Social Origins," in *Science and Christian Belief, Volume 1* (Exeter, England: Paternoster Press, 1989), 3.

frontations between creationists and evolutionists. What is not so widely known is that this confrontation is a replay of a similar encounter four centuries ago; the major difference is in the specific question under debate.[7]

In the famous historical confrontation between Galileo and the Catholic church, all the issues involved in the current creation versus evolution controversy were present: (1) If science and religion disagree, who is right? (2) Is it necessary to interpret the Bible literally when it makes reference to the natural world? (3) Does the authority of the Bible in matters relating to religion require that it be completely free of *any* kind of error on matter of which it speaks? (4) Can the Bible maintain its authority in matters of faith if it loses its authority in matters of science? The Galileo incident, when extracted from the significant political and personal milieu in which it was embedded, can serve as a paradigm for the present conflict.

At the time that Galileo argued his startling position—that the earth goes around the sun—the church was the sole authority on everything, an intellectual referee who could eliminate any idea from consideration if it didn't follow the rules. The church had, of course, developed a theology to explain scriptural and religious truth and had selectively allowed some of the secular ideas of ancient Greek philosopher Aristotle to complement this body of theological truth.

We will look briefly at some of the important leaders of the Early Church and see how their particular worldviews were based on the Bible, interpreted within the context of the reigning philosophical perspective, which was an otherworldly, nonscientific school of thought that had originated centuries earlier with Plato. And this seemed perfectly acceptable—indeed it seemed obviously correct—until certain scientific discoveries challenged some of those worldviews, which by then had come to be identified with the authority of the Bible.

For most of its history, the church has not had to deal with the challenge of science, since science is a Johnny-come-lately on the scene. As modern science emerged, it found itself fre-

---

7. See, for example, Charles Hummel, *The Galileo Connection: Resolving Conflicts Between Science and the Bible* (Downers Grove, Ill.: InterVarsity Press, 1986).

quently challenging and even undermining the very foundations on which the prevailing worldview was based.

The Prescientific Era

Modern science started sometime in the 17th century.[8] Galileo Galilei, who died in 1642, has frequently been called the first modern scientist. In considering the history of science, the centuries before Galileo can, with some oversimplification, be divided into two epochs, separated by the great medieval theologian Thomas Aquinas, who died in 1274. The 12 centuries before Aquinas were animated by spiritual concerns; it was a time of monks and monasteries and very little interest in matters of science. Sometime around the 13th century, interest in science was rekindled, and this interest eventually gave birth to modern science, when people went from being interested in science to actually *being* scientists.

In the millennium that preceded Aquinas, the natural world was viewed largely as a subordinate realm, the study of which was at best an unhealthy distraction. Then, through the reemergence of the natural philosophy of Aristotle, who lived several centuries before Christ, an interest in the natural world was restored. This reawakened interest in the natural world was not truly scientific, however, since it tended to rely almost exclusively on the authority of ancient thinkers. Instead it was a sort of scientific fundamentalism that believed all truth had already been revealed to people like Aristotle and Galen (the Roman medical expert who had gained his insight into the structure of the human body through his work with performers injured in the forums). The way to learn science was to read these ancient authorities, not to do experiments and make observations. Modern science, by contrast, recognizes only observation as its ultimate authority. There is no modern Aristotle whose authority is unquestioned. Even Einstein is widely known to have been wrong on some points.

---

8. This, of course, is an oversimplification. Galileo retained much of the medieval approach in his method. Nevertheless, he did insist that observation had to be the final authority and that it was folly to deny what could be so clearly seen with the eyes just because it seemed to contradict some theological or biblical dogma.

During the long centuries through which Western culture passed before science entered the picture, the absence of meaningful contributions from science made it difficult for these early thinkers, many of whom were quite brilliant, to produce a complete and adequate worldview. Some of them, in fact, had such otherworldly perspectives that the mere possibility of a discipline fully focused on the irrelevant details of this world was all but inconceivable. Some of them were explicitly opposed to scientific ideas, all of which were the product of pre-Christian Greece. Some of them entangled their theology with a pseudoscience that quickly became obsolete, creating additional tensions. Some of them endeavored to use the Bible as a source for scientific ideas and came up with very novel ideas about the structure of the world, such as the sixth-century notion that the universe was modeled after the tabernacle of Moses.

The problem during the Middle Ages, however, is not so much religion versus science as religion without science. The intellectual conversations of the Middle Ages took place inside a philosophical walled city, a city with a narrow gate through which certain ideas, like people with the plague, were not allowed to pass, lest they infect the health of those within the city. For the first 13 centuries of the Christian era, science was outside these walls, rarely seen, only occasionally confronted, and never embraced.

Science could not have flourished in the zealously spiritual intellectual climate of the Middle Ages. There were too many challenges. The issues involved (1) *relevance:* the pursuit of knowledge of nature was perceived to be an unhealthy distraction from the pursuit of spirituality; (2) *authority:* the Scriptures, which included the Church's traditional interpretation of them, were the only trustworthy guide in matters relating to the natural world; and even (3) *feasibility:* Plato had taught that the senses, on which science must rely, were incapable of discovering real truth.

The prevailing attitude that emerged from this era is echoed in this famous quote from that great fourth-century theologian Augustine, the bishop of Hippo: "Nothing is to be accepted save on the authority of Scripture, since that authority is greater than all the powers of the human mind." This sentiment grew in part out of Augustine's dissatisfaction with the mutually contradictory nature of the secular philosophies he had studied. In contrast, the biblical revelation seemed more coherent. Furthermore Augustine took his lead from Plato, who had taught that our limited (Augustine would say fallen) senses were inadequate to discover truth. It seemed safer to place one's trust in the authority of Scripture rather than in the philosophies of men.

Augustine himself on occasion expressed some appreciation for the classical philosophy that had emerged from Greece in the centuries before Christ. He made it clear that accurate knowledge of the natural world was superior to ignorant superstition but was still not worth pursuing. His eager followers, however, determined to walk only in his shadow, chiseled his famous quote into the granite of their monasteries, where it became a grand warning against the dangers of drinking at the well of secularism.

This worldview, in a gradually deteriorating form, lasted until the natural philosophy of Aristotle was rediscovered several centuries later and "the powers of the human mind," at least Aristotle's mind, began to be appreciated once again. But even this new synthetic worldview, which recognized two authorities and was brilliantly conceived by Thomas Aquinas, was incompatible with the discoveries made during the scientific revolution of the 16th and 17th centuries. Aquinas' medieval synthesis was an ingenious but hopelessly entangled combination of ideas extracted from Aristotle on the one hand and the Scriptures on the other. Without understanding the essence of science, Aquinas assumed that the ancient authorities had discovered just about all there was to know about the natural world and that the rest of the picture could be found in the Bible. From this dual foundation an elaborate worldview was constructed and elevated to the point of orthodoxy. Epic poems, like Dante's *Inferno*, were based on it. Magnificent stained-glass mosaics celebrated it. Universities educated students to believe it.

Unfortunately, almost all the scientific ideas the Church borrowed from Aristotle were wrong. And this became even more unfortunate as these ideas became entwined with theology until certain elements of Aristotle's philosophy were essentially church dogma.

The scientific revolution was born out of the growing conviction that the explanations of Aristotle were inadequate to account for many straightforward natural phenomena—explanations that, in many cases, had become a part of religious doctrine. The Church was forced against her will to abandon many deeply held ideas as the refining fires of the new science burned ever more brightly. The earth was displaced from the center of the universe and set adrift in a vast universe, the perfect and unchanging heavens were found to be imperfect and changing, the young earth became old, the small universe grew large, and so on. The vast territory ruled by the Church of the Middle Ages became a small plot of land defended by fearful theologians on guard against a final attack by the intellectually greedy scientists.

We shall see, however, that *none* of the founders of the new science were deliberately challenging religion. In fact, most of them—including such luminaries as Copernicus, Galileo, Kepler, and Newton—were committed Christians who felt their science was a legitimate way to worship the Creator of the universe. Unfortunately, the contemporary leaders of the religious community—powerful figures like Luther, Calvin, and assorted popes and bishops—did not agree. Practically all the important religious leaders of that period eventually attacked the new science as incompatible with the theology of their particular churches.[9]

By the time the scientific revolution had ended and science had come of age, it had acquired a position of considerable authority. By the 19th century the Church had learned, primarily from bitter experience, that there was nothing to be gained by challenging the new scientific theories and that there was credibility to be lost by constantly arguing and losing. So the Church

---

9. The Galileo affair is very complicated. At certain points Galileo had very influential church leaders on his side; but politics, pressure from Aristotelian academics (whom Galileo loved to humiliate), and personalities (Galileo was quite pigheaded) eventually led to his condemnation. This book will not attempt to present all the various intrigues; rather, it will focus primarily on the role the Church played in all of this as it became persuaded to condemn the new astronomy.

began to exercise restraint when referring to the natural world, having realized that its methods were not adequate for such investigations. Fortunately, most of the central dogmas of religion were by now outside the domain of science, so the long argument seemed to dissipate, at least for the time being.[10]

In many cases the Church responded to its constant humiliation at the hands of the scientists by turning inward.[11] If religion could be made independent of science, then there would be no more disagreement. The natural theology of the founders of modern science disappeared as the religious community convinced itself that science had nothing worthwhile to contribute to the theological discussion.

This approach was indeed successful in avoiding confrontation, but at the expense of the mutually beneficial dialogue between science and religion—a dialogue that neither party can afford to be without.

The primary concern of this book is the current controversy over origins. A group of fundamentalists calling themselves scientific creationists is insisting that all scientific theories must conform to the Scriptures—as they interpret them. They deplore secular science and insist upon a literal reading of all passages in the Bible as the needle's eye through which new scientific theories must pass.

Not much of the modern scientific worldview will fit through the needle's eye. Under attack are the current scientific explanations of (1) the age of the earth, (2) continental drift, (3) the origin of the solar system, (4) the formation of stars, (5) the origin of life, (6) the extinction of the dinosaurs, (7) the formation of fossils, (8) Einstein's theory of relativity, (9) the constancy of the speed of light, and (10) the origin of humanity. The list could be expanded almost indefinitely.

---

10. It is interesting to note that science essentially died in Italy after the Galileo incident and was reborn in England with Isaac Newton. Unbridled intellectual freedom is a prerequisite for a strong science, which is why science has always been so strong in the United States. There are those who would curtail this freedom, however.

11. It is interesting to note that the Church's response to the Darwinian challenge was much less dramatic than the earlier response to Galileo, even though Darwin's ideas cut much closer to the heart of religion. This is probably due in some small part to the lessons the Church learned earlier, but it also reflects the dramatically different role the Church was playing in society at the time of Darwin.

To some degree, the conflict revives a centuries-old confrontation between the authority of science and the authority of the Bible.

If we review the confrontation between Galileo and the Church, we may find that history is repeating itself.

A Lesson from History

One important outcome of the Galileo incident was the recognition that science and religion are two distinct fields of inquiry. They are not individually capable of addressing all questions about reality. In fact, as we saw in the first chapter, a satisfactory worldview requires the dynamic synthesis of many authorities. As Galileo liked to quip, "The Bible teaches us how to go to heaven, not how the heavens go." This bit of wisdom summarizes the perspective that most scientists and theologians now share on this once troubling question. And for many contemporary thinkers, science and religion provide complementary perspectives on the world, jointly contributing to a very satisfying worldview that comfortably embraces both authorities: (1) the findings of modern science are accepted, which results in a reverential appreciation for the beauty, order, and greatness of the universe, and (2) religion gives this appreciation expression in the form of praise for the Creator. This is the Galilean dogma.

Galileo argued that religious dogmas must not be allowed to contradict observation. While this is accepted almost universally today, it was controversial at the time Galileo proposed it. When Galileo looked through his telescope and saw spots on the sun, his critics disputed his discoveries. There could not be spots on the sun, they argued, because the sun must be perfect, without spot or blemish. With similar logic, the religious and even scientific authorities disputed his discovery of the satellites of Jupiter, the surface features of the moon, and so on. When Galileo suggested that his critics simply look through the telescope for themselves, they responded that reality was not to be determined by looking through an instrument. Such an instrument was a tool of the devil and they, unlike Galileo, were not going to be led astray by it.

Galileo's famous confrontation came when he insisted that his discoveries demonstrated the truth of the controversial new Copernican astronomy: the earth was indeed moving around the sun, not vice versa. When Galileo promoted this heretical thesis in a number of very popular writings, ecclesiastical hackles began to rise. Galileo was arrested, threatened with torture, forced to recant, and prevented from continuing in his scientific studies.

Recently the Roman Catholic church has acknowledged its error in the handling of the Galileo affair. An apology has been issued. The Galilean dogma has now officially supplanted the obsolete perspective that ruled for so many centuries. The present pope regularly engages in dialogue with members of the scientific community so that a similar affair will not occur again.

The Galilean dogma clearly states that there must be a distinction between the focus of science and the focus of religion. The Bible, or religion, deals with how to go to heaven (which can be enlarged metaphorically to include the various spiritual interests of the Church); science deals with how the heavens go. Science is thus discouraged from making pronouncements on religious questions, and religion is discouraged from making pronouncements on scientific questions.

But what is a scientific question? Where is the boundary between science and religion? Is the shape of the earth to be determined by science? What about the position of the earth? What about the age of the earth? What about the origin of life? What about the sinful nature of man?

It is not a simple matter to locate the boundary between a scientific question and a religious one. History records the constant adjustment of this boundary as (1) the ability of science to address an increasingly larger sphere of questions about the universe expanded until it encroached upon territory once governed by religion and (2) the ability of religious scholars to understand the implication of how the biblical message grew until they were convinced that the Bible was not trying to teach science.

The Unholy War

We will argue that there should not be any disagreement between science and religion. They are sufficiently distinct so that they do not need to provide *the same kind of explanations for the same phenomenon.* They may very well observe and be interested in the same phenomenon, but their interests are not at the same level. It is thus possible for science and religion both to be authoritative without coming into conflict.

Unfortunately, a few polemicists would have us believe otherwise. Some science writers feel it necessary to wage war on religion. Pretending to represent the scientific community, they are able to persuade some people that religion is the enemy of science.

On the side of religion, a group calling themselves scientific creationists is attempting to return to a long-discredited approach to the Bible, namely that it can be a sourcebook for science, superior in every way to conventional scientific sources. This group feels it necessary to wage war on modern science. Arguing that it is possible to discover scientific truths such as the age of the earth from the Bible, they have persuaded some people that science is the enemy of religion.[12]

Both of these positions represent minority viewpoints. Most scientists do not feel religion should be discarded; most Christians do not feel science is conspiring to overthrow religion.

Looking Ahead

The next two chapters will deal with some of the historical issues that provide useful background for the current controversy. We will see that it has always been difficult to balance the respective authorities of science and religion. From the fall of Rome (in 476) through the Middle Ages the Church was the sole authority in matters spiritual as well as those relating to descriptions of the natural world. After Aquinas, the authority of Aristotle was added to that of Scripture. During the scientific revolution beginning in the 17th century, the authority of reli-

---

12. An increasing number of scientists are, in fact, becoming adversaries of religion as the religious antiscientific movement grows to the point at which prominent scientists feel the need to respond. There is now a scientific organization called the "National Center for Science Education," whose sole purpose is to refute the claims of the scientific creationists. It is interesting to note that this organization promotes books written by evangelical scientists who argue that scientific creationism is neither good science nor good religion.

gion (and Aristotle) was replaced by that of science in dealing with questions about nature.

Chapter 3 will discuss the perspective that the founders of modern science developed on this issue. We will see that, without exception, they all felt their science was compatible with the profound Christian faith they shared. In fact, they argued that their science was actually complementary to their faith, enriching their understanding of God and His creation. They were all comfortable with what we call natural theology, which is based on the belief that God has indeed revealed himself through nature and that His existence can be inferred or even proved from the details and patterns evident in that nature.

Chapter 4 will discuss the response of the Church to the developing new science. We will see that the Church, having adopted the inadequate explanations of Aristotle, which were gradually being demonstrated to be wrong, reacted initially with considerable hostility. Some of the early scientists were condemned as heretics, at least one was put to death, and many of their writings were placed on the *Index*—a catalog of forbidden books containing dangerous material that good Christians were forbidden to read.

The Church put up a valiant but futile struggle to maintain its grip on the authority that it had held without challenge for 15 centuries. Gradually and painfully, this authority eroded as the Church was forced to share it with the new science. The intellectual alliance that was forced upon the Church, however, was an uneasy one and witnessed numerous attempts by both parties to usurp the throne and assert unilateral authority. It was, alas, a marriage made on earth and not in heaven.

3

The Receding Creator

. . . . .

History teaches us that man learns nothing from History.

Georg W. F. Hegel

. . . . .

Prologue: Of Numbers and Ideas

Five centuries before Christ, an unfortunate Greek mathematician named Hippasos released to the world a terrible secret. Breaking the solemn oath of secrecy that bound the members of his group of radical mathematicians, he let it be known that not all numbers could be written as simple fractions. Some numbers, he said, such as pi, could not be written as one whole number divided by another.

This extraordinary discovery could only mean one thing: the world was not composed of pure whole numbers as Hippasos and his comrades in math had believed and taught. With the discovery of this terrible truth, the elaborate mathematical worldview of ancient Greece crumbled to the ground. For his role in its demise, the angry gods, according to legend, sent Hippasos to a watery grave.

An obscure Greek mathematician, Hippasos was a follower of Pythagoras, who is well known for his theorem about triangles. This theorem, central to the branch of mathematics known as geometry, is called Pythagorean theorem[1] and is generally encountered somewhere in high school.

---

1. Pythagorean theorem states that the length of the long side of a triangle, called the hypotenuse, can be determined from a knowledge of the lengths of the other two sides. ($C^2 = A^2 + B^2$, where A and B are the lengths of the two short sides and C is the

Pythagoras was one of the first thinkers in the Western tradition. He lived several centuries before Christ was born and originated an influential school of thought that came to be known, not surprisingly, as Pythagoreanism. The Pythagoreans, as his followers were creatively named, believed whole numbers (1, 2, 3, etc.) were the key to understanding the universe. They discovered, for example, that there were interesting numerical relationships that determined the tones produced by vibrating strings, such as those on guitars or violins. They believed that the regular motion of the heavenly bodies produced such musical tones, which they called the "music of the spheres." They discovered that much of nature seemed to resonate with the harmony and symmetry characteristic of mathematics.

The Pythagoreans were very enthusiastic about their insights into the mathematic aspects of nature. To emphasize the importance of these discoveries, they established a school in Italy that was practically a religious sect organized around the veneration of numbers. The school had secret initiation ceremonies, religious vows, and an overall philosophy that was to govern all aspects of the lives of its members. The Pythagoreans were mathematical priests, and Pythagoras was their bishop.

The Pythagoreans became so enamored with their insights into the importance of numbers that they began to exaggerate the role of numbers in the universe. Abstract notions like love and justice became associated with specific numbers: 2 was opinion, 8 was love, justice was a square number like 4 or 9, and so on. Pythagoras "preached like an inspired prophet that all nature, the entire universe in fact, physical, metaphysical, mental, moral, mathematical—*everything*—is built on the discrete pattern of the integers 1, 2, 3, . . . and is interpretable in terms of these God-given bricks alone; God, he declared, is 'number.'"[2] Number, argued Pythagoras, was the key to understanding everything in the universe, as he developed a bizarre mathe-

---

length of the long side of a triangle that has one right angle.) The theorem is an example of deductive thinking, which produces absolutely certain conclusions from premises. In deduction there is no possibility of error in the reasoning process, although the initial premises can be in error.

2. E. T. Bell, *Men of Mathematics* (New York: Simon and Schuster, 1965), 21.

matical metaphysics that seems quite foreign to the modern mind.

This myopic attempt to focus on number as the key to explaining everything in the universe led them to a very distorted description of reality. Reality is far too complex to be reduced to a simple jigsaw puzzle of numbers. By attempting to do so, Pythagoras was prevented from ever developing a comprehensive worldview that could address reality in a meaningful way. In his own lifetime, in fact, the disastrous discovery of the so-called irrational numbers[3] mentioned above showed him the error of his assumptions.

The mathematical tree of knowledge, planted and nurtured by the Pythagoreans, did not grow to fill the universe as they had anticipated. The universe is not constructed entirely from whole numbers; it is not constructed from numbers at all, at least not in the sense that Pythagoras believed. But Pythagoras can serve as a *symbol* of the new way the Greeks were looking at the world. At a time when other civilizations were listening to nature and hearing the angry and discordant roar of the gods, the Greeks were beginning to hear the music of the spheres.[4]

Pythagoras lived in the century that gave birth to Western civilization. He, and thinkers like him, were the midwives that brought forth a brand-new way of looking at the world, one that began to abandon mythology and replace it with science. At first their ideas were crude and primitive, but their way of thinking about nature—rational speculation attempting to understand observed phenomena—started Western civilization on its long climb to our modern scientific worldview.

Outline

The theme of this chapter is the gradual dethronement of religion as the primary authority in understanding the natural world. As Western society progressed from primitive Christian-

---

3. Irrational numbers are numbers that cannot be expressed as simple fractions. Pi and the square root of two are common examples of irrational numbers. They cannot be written in any simple way, and, in fact, they cannot be completely written down at all because they have an infinite series of numbers required for their representation.

4. The Greek notion of the music of the spheres is reminiscent of the reference in Job 38:7 to the morning stars singing together.

ity, through the Middle Ages, through the Renaissance, and finally to the Enlightenment, science grew from irrelevant to dominant, while religion did exactly the reverse, in terms of the importance accorded it in understanding the natural world.

Remarkably, however, even though the new science was clearly replacing a long-standing religious authority, the founders of the new science—Copernicus, Kepler, Galileo, and Newton—did not feel that their replacement of theological explanations (angels pushing planets) with scientific ones (gravity moving planets) in any way diminished faith in God as the Creator. In fact, they felt their science was fundamentally theological, enhancing their understanding of God.

The attitude of many religious authorities toward science, however, was quite different. It was one of resentment and even hostility as many theologians and Church leaders were unable to adapt their personal worldviews to accommodate the new view of the universe being developed by the science of the time.

To make matters worse, the medieval worldview, which was the intellectual legacy of the centuries that preceded the development of modern science, seemed to have an extraordinary veneer of permanence; it possessed a finality that made it appear invulnerable to change. But the winds of change blew hard, and eventually even the stationary earth of the Middle Ages was loosed from its moorings and set into motion around the sun, following an impersonal and calculable pattern. It seemed as though God was less and less involved in the creation, and eventually a philosophical perspective developed that preached God was not involved in any way with His creation. He was not moving the planets around the sun, He was not turning acorns into oaks, and He was not paying any attention to the mundane affairs of tiny creatures clinging to the sides of the third planet out from a medium-sized star called the sun.

(The emphasis of this chapter and the next is on the lessons of history, rather than on history itself. The material is organized so that certain time periods are discussed more than once, from different perspectives and with different purposes.)

The Development of the Medieval Worldview
Platonic Roots: The World Is a Shadow

When Christianity began, it was an insignificant movement. By A.D. 320 it had become the official religion of Rome, and its ideas were flowing at an ever-increasing rate into the larger stream of ideas that traced their origins back to the rocky, windswept shores of Greece, the intellectual wellspring of Western civilization. This wellspring was an intellectual golden age in which pure thinkers like Pythagoras, Socrates, Plato, and Aristotle—who have come to symbolize and encapsulate that period of genius—were citizens of great importance. Plato and Aristotle, in particular, exerted an enormous influence on the development of Western civilization, an influence that can still be felt.

Plato embraced a philosophical tradition that had very little appreciation for observation of the natural world. He taught that we must try to focus on purely theoretical notions, abstractions that revealed themselves only to the mind. While many of the Greek philosophers who preceded Plato had been quite interested in what we would call physics, they had been unable to develop a consensus about the nature of the physical world as it appeared to the senses. The failure of these early scientists— Anaximander, Anaximines, Empedocles, Anaxagoras, Leucippus, Democritus—to come to any agreement convinced Plato that their assumptions must have been fundamentally in error.

Thus, in agreement with the philosopher Heraclitus, source of the oft-quoted phrase "nothing is constant save change," Plato came to believe that nature was a constantly changing world that could yield no certain knowledge through observation. The error of the scientists, argued Plato, was in their assumption that truth about the natural world could be discovered via the senses through observation. So Plato believed and taught that there could be no such thing as a scientific method and no point in approaching the world from that perspective.

Among Plato's many writings—which include a great variety of very important books—only one, a dialogue called *Timaeus* (after one of the characters in the dialogue), is concerned to any great degree with natural science. And even this work makes it clear that nature is not to be understood through observation, but rather through reason. "The world," argues Timaeus, "has been framed in the likeness of that which is apprehended by reason and mind and is unchangeable, and must therefore . . . be a copy of something."[5] Thus, being an imperfect copy, the sensible world was not a source for truth but only subjective opinions about what might lie beyond the observed copy. And what is the point of science if the end product is but opinion?

Plato devoted his efforts to the development of a theory of knowledge that would allow for the possibility of absolute knowledge, which was certainly to be preferred to mere opinion. This absolute knowledge, however, resided only in the eternal, changeless realities that existed in a transcendent realm beyond the natural world. This transcendent realm was the world of the "forms," a philosophical heaven where no one sees through a glass darkly.

The world of the forms was real; this world, where we have been assigned to live, is but a copy or a shadow of the real world. Plato's philosophy, developed in pagan Greece centuries before Christ, thus contained a theoretical framework that seemed designed to complement the theology of the developing Christian tradition, which was extremely interested in better worlds beyond this imperfect and fallen one.

Plato's philosophy stood in stark contrast to that of the more scientifically minded Aristotle, his superstar student. While Aristotle, who was almost a scientist, had his moment in the philosophical sun, it was Plato's philosophy that was to win the first round and grow to dominate the first centuries of the Christian era. And, as Plato's star rose ever higher in the intellectual firmament, it eventually overwhelmed Aristotle and led to a widespread loss of interest in Aristotle's primitive scientific notions. Eventually the works of Aristotle found themselves relegated to rare libraries where they grew dusty and brittle as the centuries passed, their pages opened by only the occasional student. Christian thinkers, listening for the voice of philosophy to clarify their faith, heard only Plato and his successors.

---

5. Plato's Timaeus in *The Dialogues of Plato,* quoted in Jefferson Hane Weaver, *The World of Physics: A Small Library of the Literature of Physics from Antiquity to the Present* (New York: Simon and Schuster, 1987), 1:282.

Augustine: Christianity Embraces the Shadows

Plato and Aristotle represent a fork in the philosophical road, and deep thinkers throughout history have frequently had to make a decision to leave one or the other of them behind. Great intellectual movements can sometimes be identified by which of these two philosophers they chose to embrace. One such thinker confronted with this decision was Augustine, Christendom's first intellectual giant, a powerful and influential figure who, seemingly singlehandedly, shaped the worldview of the latter half of the first millennium.

Augustine was born in 354 in the midst of a century that was witnessing the consolidation of the power of the Christian Church as an institution and the ongoing development of an orthodoxy. His mother was a Christian, and his father was a pagan. He was raised in a highly intellectual environment, which eventually led the young philosopher into the maze of local pagan religions searching for meaning. He eventually found his way out of the maze and embraced Christianity, which he had first encountered at his mother's knee. Augustine became recognized as one of the most profound thinkers in the history of Christianity and is credited with making an incalculable and lasting contribution to the development of the Church, both theologically and politically.

One commentator puts it this way:

> In him the Western Church produced its first towering intellect—and indeed its last for another 600 years . . . What he was to mean for the future can only be indicated. All the men who had to bring Europe through the next six or seven centuries fed upon him. We see Pope Gregory the Great at the end of the sixth century reading and rereading the *Confessions*. We see the Emperor Charlemagne at the end of the eighth century using the *City of God* as a kind of Bible.[6]

Augustine took his philosophical cue from Plato after many years of deep searching. Specifically, he embraced the philosophy known as Neoplatonism, a derivative of Platonism

---

6. F. J. Sheed, trans., *The Confessions of St. Augustine* (New York: Sheed and Ward, 1943), vi.

developed by Plotinus. Where Plato had argued that the study of nature was unproductive, Plotinus argued that it was unhealthy, further diminishing the already low status that Plato had accorded it. In fact, Plotinus himself had such a low opinion of the natural world that he is said to "have blushed because he had a body,"[7] as if he would have preferred the more modest existence of a disembodied spirit.

Neoplatonism taught that the universe was a hierarchy of different levels, with God at the top. Reality was a "graded series from the divine to the material, and man, who has in him some part of the divine, longs for union with the eternal source of things."[8] For a Neoplatonist the empirical world of the senses—the world that fascinated Aristotle—was an inferior, shadowy, imperfect reality, many levels below the divine. To focus on this inferior world was to be distracted from the pursuit of wholeness, to look down rather than up. "Like the other men of his time, Plotinus found this world a sea of troubles and a vale of tears; like them he sought to leave it; and like them he found perfect peace only in otherworldliness."[9]

Augustine had wandered for many years in Plotinus' vale of tears. He longed for his soul to be united with the Creator from whence it had emerged, and he wrote deeply and profoundly about the mechanics of that quest. Plotinus' Neoplatonism turned out to be the path that led Augustine out of the vale of tears and into the light of the Christianity that he had first learned from his mother. His troubled soul found the rest for which it had so long been seeking, as if it had, at last, come home.

Out of these profound experiences Augustine created the "first philosophical exposition of Christianity,"[10] in which he argued forcefully that anything that might distract the soul from its quest for God must be avoided. Augustine argued eloquently and well—so well that his personal theology was capable of sustaining six centuries of Christendom while Europe collapsed

7. Arthur Koestler, *The Sleepwalkers* (New York: Macmillan Co., 1959), 86.

8. W. L. Reese, *Dictionary of Philosophy and Religion* (Atlantic Highlands, N.J.: Humanities Press), 385.

9. W. T. Jones, *The Medieval Mind: A History of Western Philosophy* (New York: Harcourt Brace Jovanovich, 1969), 18.

10. Ibid., 75.

into ruin around it. He was "to a greater degree than any emperor or barbarian warlord, a maker of history and a builder of the bridge which was to lead from the old world to the new."[11]

But bridges are narrow and have room for but limited traffic. The bridge that Augustine built was too narrow for many of the ideas that could have crossed from classical to medieval Europe. And so the primitive ideas of Greek science, perceived as but a distraction from the soul's search for God, were turned away. "Let Thales depart with his water, Anaximines with the air, the Stoics with their fire, Epicurus with his atoms,"[12] insisted Augustine in *The City of God*, as he labored to quarantine those ideas that might infect the Christian Church with the disease of curiosity.

The Dark Ages: The World in Shadow

The philosophy of Augustine and his followers led, quite naturally, to a subordination of the study of the physical world. This unfortunate development sent science, which was still struggling to be born, back into the womb, where it remained for a thousand years.

Those who love science tend to view the early Middle Ages as a gloomy period, dominated as they were by Neoplatonism and the purely spiritual focus of the Church. These Dark Ages,[13] as they are called, started about 500 years after Christ and lasted several centuries—centuries that saw the potentially magnificent edifice of science started in Greece a millennium earlier crumble and disintegrate through both attack and neglect. The

---

11. Christopher Dawson, quoted in foreword to *The Confessions of St. Augustine* (see note 6 on p. 66).

12. Bertrand Russell, *A History of Western Philosophy* (New York: Simon and Schuster, 1945), 358. Russell has paraphrased Augustine a bit. The actual passage in *The City of God* (Chap. 5 of Book 8) is somewhat less dramatic. It is clear, however, that Augustine had very little time for non-Platonists.

13. It is not universally acknowledged that the Dark Ages were actually all that "dark." The pejorative label for this period was coined by a later generation in an act of self-congratulation. In the history of science, however, the Dark Ages represent a long period that contains nothing of relevance. A brief survey of science will start with Aristotle in the 5th century B.C. (or perhaps Thales), proceed to Ptolemy (2nd century A.D.), and then to Copernicus (16th century A.D.), jumping over the long period called the Dark Ages. When Copernicus began his work in astronomy it was in response to Ptolemy, who had died more than 13 centuries earlier.

followers of Augustine[14] retreated to monasteries in remote locations as if to escape somehow from the distraction of actually
living in the real world. The real world, after all, was only valuable to the extent that it pointed toward a more important spiritual reality. Theology, as the study of the highest form of knowledge, became known as the queen of the sciences.

Whatever progress had been made in science was set aside.
In astronomy, for example, the symmetrical and orderly universe of Aristotle was spiritualized to such an extent that even
its physical structure must somehow reveal religious truth.

As these various philosophical ideas took hold, the scientific spirit that had animated Aristotle and his followers was gradually extracted from Christendom until it seemed that there was
but one lonely scholar trying to hold on to Aristotle's approach
to the natural world. His name was Boethius, and he eventually
ended up in jail because of political misfortune. Called the last
classical scholar, having transmitted Aristotle's logic to the Middle Ages, he was eventually executed. With his passing, Aristotle's spirit of scientific inquiry within Christendom became comatose until being revived six long centuries later. Referring to
this unfortunate episode in the history of science, a modern
scholar has lamented:

> Boethius was executed in 524, and with the extin
> guishing of that last guttering lamp the darkness closed
> in. The climate during the Dark Ages grew literally cold
> er, as if the sun itself had lost interest in the mundane . . .
> The stars came down: Conservative churchmen modeled
> the universe after the tabernacle of Moses; as the taberna
> cle was a tent, the sky was demoted from a glorious
> sphere to its prior status as a low tent roof. The planets,
> they said, were pushed around by angels . . . the proud

---

14. To be fair to Augustine, whose intellect and influence rank with the best in the
Western tradition, there was no real "science" in his world. He did not explicitly reject
science; he simply failed to extend the primitive ideas that were germinating during his
lifetime. And of course, it must be emphasized that a theologian has no obligation to
promote science any more than scientists have some obligation to promote theology.
Furthermore, Augustine's followers, the "Augustinians," tended to exaggerate his reservations about the value of science. In the final analysis, the secondary role assigned to
science during the Middle Ages finds its origin in ancient Greece, centuries before the
start of the Christian era.

round earth was hammered flat; likewise the shimmering sun. Behind the sky reposed eternal Heaven, accessible only through death.[15]

The Medieval Synthesis: Aristotle Reincarnated

The period called the Dark Ages eventually ended. The spiritual universe of Augustine began to shrink ever so slightly, creating some room for a fresh perspective. This fresh perspective was provided sometime in the 12th century, not by some new and revolutionary thinker but by the rediscovery of the old perspective of Aristotle.

Once again philosophy found itself at the same Plato/Aristotle fork in the philosophical road. A different mind-set prevailed this time, and the long-forsaken Aristotle was embraced, and with more enthusiasm than Plato had ever received. After some initial and hostile reaction, the primitive science of Aristotle was eventually adopted by the Church and fused into a coherent worldview by Thomas Aquinas, who lived in the 13th century. The result was a powerful synthesis in which many of Aristotle's scientific ideas were elevated to the level of theology. Aquinas' systematic and far-reaching synthesis of the revelation of Christianity and the reason of Aristotle was to exert an extraordinary influence on the development of Catholic thought through subsequent centuries. In fact, it was precisely this development, discussed in detail in the next chapter, that forms the background of the Galileo affair.

The Renaissance

The embracing of Aristotle by the Church and the subsequent legitimization and then sanctification of his science was only one of many elements that were combining synergistically to create the Renaissance. Centuries of what, in hindsight, looks like intolerable intellectual boredom were being transformed by that great enthusiasm we call the Renaissance.

---

15. Timothy Ferris, *Coming of Age in the Milky Way* (New York: William Morrow and Co., 1988), 44.

The Renaissance started in the late 13th century with a rekindled interest in many aspects of the culture developed in centuries before Christ. The remarkable achievements of the Greeks, who included Pythagoras, Socrates, Aristarchus, and Plato, as well as Aristotle, appeared like cultural and intellectual beacons to a society that had been sitting stagnant for centuries, trying to avoid thinking about anything that might pose a problem for their medieval worldview. The collective intelligence of a society that had been tethered by the Middle Ages' short intellectual chain was suddenly unleashed.

Intellectual giants now roamed free, searching boldly for new ideas, first in the writings of ancient Greeks like Aristarchus and Aristotle, and then within the uncharted territory of their own fertile imaginations. Copernicus, Galileo, Kepler, Newton, and Laplace, like children in a new sandbox, built a new universe, one ruled by physical laws, not spiritual ones. The scientist began to replace the theologian as the primary architect of the physical universe.

From Theism to Deism

Society's vision of the physical universe was dramatically altered, led by an aggressive new science that was confidently charting new waters. Science acquired new authority in the description of nature as the old mode of description, with its emphasis on orthodoxy, was displaced. The new universe, it seemed, was ruled by natural law, not spiritual beings. The God that so fully animated the world of the Middle Ages found himself with a continuously shrinking job description in the new scheme of things. For Copernicus, the first astronomer of the scientific revolution, God was personally responsible for all the activity in the heavens; for Laplace, at the other end of the revolution, God was an irrelevant hypothesis, absolutely uninvolved in the creation.

The growth of science from Copernicus to Laplace convinced many that the universe could indeed run by itself; natural law seemed to be more than competent to keep things on course, and the planet-pushing angels of the Dark Ages joined the gods of ancient Greece in the graveyard of mythology. Finally, it seemed, there was nothing at all left for God to do in the universe. He had been reduced to a Watchmaker who produced beautiful watches that kept perfect time, never needed to be wound, and never broke down.

Deism is the name of the mechanical Watchmaker worldview, where God has nothing more important to do than keep the planets from veering off course. A central tenet of Deism, and perhaps the only one that is of interest in this context, is the notion that "God, as First Cause, created the universe but then left it to run on its own. God is thus not immanent, not fully personal, not sovereign over human affairs, not providential."[16]

Deism was the inevitable conclusion to a philosophy convinced that natural law is the only key to unlocking the secrets of the universe. Like the Pythagoreans two millennia before them, the devotees of the new order allowed but a single authority, that of natural law, and found themselves in an inhospitable universe of their own design.

In the years following Newton, the new worldview expanded the scope of natural law until many became convinced that it was the only light that could be used to illuminate the physical universe. As the methods of science were successfully applied to an increasingly larger range of phenomenon, the significance of science grew until some philosophers aimed the coldly analytical weapons of science at religion. The spiritual universe of Augustine, which the Renaissance had unconsciously merged with the developing scientific perspective, was extracted and discarded. Determined that natural law was the only source of authority in the quest for a worldview, they insisted that there was no room for special revelation from God, such as could be found in the Bible. The revelation of God in nature was more than adequate.

From Deism to Naturalism

The developing intellectual perspective on the nature of reality expanded the role of natural law until eventually there was no room in the universe for God. By the time the great

---

16. Sire, *Universe Next Door*, 51.

French mathematician Pierre-Simon de Laplace wrote his books on astronomy at the beginning of the 19th century, it was no longer fashionable to include God within a comprehensive description of the universe. The famous French general, Napoleon Bonaparte, who was a patron of Laplace, chided him: "They tell me you have written this large book on the system of the universe, and have never even mentioned its Creator." Laplace defended himself with his now-famous reply, "I had no need of that hypothesis." Theology was no longer the queen of the sciences. In fact, the queen was now officially in retreat, convinced that it was foolhardy to continue this conversation with the aggressive and opinionated new science. (There are, however, encouraging signs that this conversation is being rejuvenated.[17])

Laplace's universe was a big machine. It was thoroughly mechanical with all its mechanical parts governed in the smallest detail by natural law. Human beings, for all their lofty philosophizing about having been "created in the image of God," were nothing more than cogs in the huge machine, twisting and turning according to laws and conditions that had been laid down when the cosmic machine was designed. Humanity's pitiful presence in the clockwork universe was of no more significance than that of stones in a stream; human history was just the bubbling of the cosmic stream as it slowly ground the stones to sediment.

The Vacant Universe

Laplace's distorted worldview was the natural consequence of an overemphasis upon the role of law in the universe. Laplace was enamored with Newton's successful efforts to discover the laws that govern the motion of the heavenly bodies. In fact, Laplace was just echoing the sentiments of his generation, a generation that practically worshiped Newton and, by extension, the power of the human intellect. The poet Alexander Pope put it eloquently:

---

17. See, for example, John Polkinghorne, *Science and Creation: The Search for Understanding* (Boston: New Science Library, 1989). Polkinghorne is an Anglican priest who used to be a theoretical physicist. The New Science Library, of which this book is a part, has as its goal "the enrichment of both the scientific and spiritual view of the world through their mutual dialogue and exchange."

Nature and Nature's laws lay hid in night:
God said, Let Newton be! and all was light.

The belief that the human intellect was capable, through science, of discovering all relevant truth about the universe invigorated the new intellectual order. What need was there for God to reveal himself? If He was there, the intellectuals would find Him. Where Augustine humbly knelt in awe before the Creator, Laplace shook his fist at the universe and defied the Creator to display himself.

Laplace's book on the universe was a watershed in the history of physical science. It indicated the end of "God as a scientific hypothesis." No longer was it acceptable to include references to the Creator in books about the creation. Copernicus, the first astronomer of the Renaissance, was a priest. Newton, who lived two centuries later, also had a profound faith in God, although his followers tended toward deism. But less than a century later Laplace wrote an obituary for the "Retired Architect" of the deistic universe. A God with nothing to do is no God at all.

The universe had become vacant.

The Faith of the Scientific Fathers

The centuries that separate Augustine, with his spiritual universe, and Laplace, with his mechanical one, saw the tension between science and religion emerge and grow. The great intellects of that important era were constantly challenged to maintain a balance between the historical authority of the Christian tradition and the impressive achievements of the new science. Like enemies in an old Western movie, the town (or in this case the universe) just wasn't big enough for the both of them.

The troubled relationship between science and religion during the period just described was the result of a simplistic or even careless interpretation of the role that God is supposed to play in the universe and in the explanation of that universe.

When Copernicus first proposed that perhaps the sun, and not the earth, was the center of the universe, he was laying the foundation for a radical new astronomy. This new astronomy was one that would certainly challenge all of the authorities of the day, religious and secular. Copernicus, however, was a devout priest with absolutely no intention of diminishing the Creator in any way. In fact, Copernicus approached his astronomy as a sort of natural theology, a way of learning about the Creator by studying the creation.

Copernicus' radical ideas were contained in his book *On the Revolutions of the Heavenly Spheres*, which was published in 1543, the year of his death. This remarkable book makes frequent references to God as the Creator. It is clear that Copernicus sees his science as an attempt to understand and appreciate the God who was responsible for the extraordinary organization of the universe. Almost five centuries ago he wrote:

> For who while intent upon things which he sees to be established in the best possible arrangement and directed by divine ordinance would not . . . be impelled towards the best, and would not feel wonder for the Maker of all, in Whom is all happiness and every good thing? For would it not have been in vain for the divine psalmist to say that he delighted in the creations of God and in the works of His hands if we were not led by these means as if by some conveyance to the contemplation of the highest good?[18]

Throughout his work, Copernicus affirmed without reservation that all the planets were moved in their regular orbits by a watchful and caring God. The regularity he was discovering was a manifestation of the faithfulness of a loving Creator. The order he discovered in his new sun-centered universe was simply the order created and maintained by God. When Copernicus watched the moon cross the sky on a clear night, he praised the Creator for moving it so regularly.

Copernicus received the proof pages of his revolutionary book while he was on his deathbed. He had waited, quite literally, until the last minute to publish *On the Revolution of the Heavenly Spheres*. Ideas he had developed decades earlier had been circulated only among close friends, because he feared the Church's response. This proved to be a prudent caution. There was indeed a powerful reaction to his challenge of the astronomical status quo. The Church taught that the earth must be

---

18. Nicolaus Copernicus, *On the Revolutions of the Heavenly Spheres*, trans. A. M. Duncan (New York: Barnes Noble Books, 1976), 35.

stationary and at the center of the universe. With Scripture[19] and tradition[20] as their authorities, they could *prove* that Copernicus' new astronomy was contrary to the faith. (We will return to this in a later chapter.)

The Copernican torch was carried enthusiastically into the midst of the emerging scientific revolution by two of the founders of modern science, Kepler and Galileo.

Johannes Kepler was an extraordinary intellect whose successes in life seem to have been restricted solely to astronomy. He had attempted without success to become a Lutheran minister, his marriage was a dismal failure, and he was considered somewhat of a social buffoon because of his odd manner of speaking and dress. Nevertheless, his efforts in astronomy laid the foundation for Isaac Newton's theory of gravity.

Kepler was also a devout Christian. When he discovered the planetary laws that now bear his name, he bowed humbly before the Creator and offered thanks that he had been the one God had chosen to discover the remarkable patterns hidden in the motion of the planets. Kepler published his discoveries in *Mysterium Cosmographicum*, which, being translated, is *The Secret of the Universe*. In this influential book, published in 1621, Kepler makes it clear that the focus of his studies is the worship of God the Creator.

> Here we are concerned with the book of nature, so greatly celebrated in sacred writings. It is in this that Paul proposes to the Gentiles that they should contemplate God like the Sun in water or in a mirror. Why then as Christians should we take any less delight in its contemplation, since it is for us with true worship to honor God, to venerate him, to wonder at him? The more rightly we understand the nature and scope of what our God has founded, the more devoted the spirit in which that is done.[21]

---

19. See, for example, Ps. 93:1 for a typical biblical reference used to proof-text a stationary earth.

20. The great medieval theologian Thomas Aquinas had stated that the earth must be at the center of the universe in his monumental *Summa Theologica*, the standard systematic theology of the day, and the foundation for most of the doctrines of the Roman Catholic church.

21. Johannes Kepler, *Mysterium Cosmographicum, The Secret of the Universe*, trans. A. M. Duncan (New York: Abaris Books, 1981), 53.

Kepler continues in the above vein for some length, emphasizing that *good science is good theology.*

A contemporary of Kepler and the primary focus of the historical quarrel between science and religion was the remarkable
Galileo Galilei, who is considered by many to be the first truly
modern scientist. Galileo was an eternal adolescent; his life can
be summarized as a continual struggle against authority, both
religious and secular. Nowhere is the conflict between authorities more clearly enunciated than in the details of Galileo's challenge of the medieval worldview.

For all his quarreling with the Church—to which we will
return later—Galileo remained a devout Christian until he died.
He grieved that the Church he loved so dearly was not comfortable with the new science. He argued eloquently for what is
now widely recognized as the only legitimate approach to the
Scriptures—that they not be read as textbooks of science from
which to extract information like the age of the earth and the
configuration of the planets.

And Galileo was also clear on the theological dimension of
his scientific efforts. The light of his science was intended to illuminate the work of the Creator. The inspiration that came
from studying the creation was really coming from the Creator.
Science and theology were one.

Galileo was the first astronomer to use a telescope. In 1610
he published some of his telescopic discoveries in a small book
titled *The Starry Messenger,* which he dedicated to a local politi-
cian, the Grand Duke of Tuscany. In the dedication of the book,
Galileo suggests that the duke should recognize the theological
dimension of his discoveries. "Accept then, most clement
Prince, the gentle glory reserved by the stars for you. May you
long enjoy those blessings which are sent to you *not so much
from the stars as from God,* their Maker and their governor."[22]

By the standards of today, Galileo was a reverent scientist.
The contemporary Church would applaud his recognition of the
Creator. By the standards of the 17th century, however, he was a
heretic. He died in 1642, blind, under house arrest, and forbid-

---

22. Stillman Drake, *Ideas and Opinions of Galileo* (New York: Doubleday, 1957), 26,
emphasis added.

den to continue the scientific studies that had given him such pleasure over the course of his productive and troubled life.

On Christmas Day in the year of Galileo's death, Isaac Newton was born, as if to announce that Galileo had not died in vain. The baton of scientific leadership passed smoothly from one genius to another as the scientific revolution found itself yet another champion. The eye of the scientific storm, however, moved from Italy to England, far beyond the reach of the Roman Catholic church.

Like his illustrious predecessors, Isaac Newton was also a Christian. As a member of the Anglican church, he was involved in a number of typical church projects, including the distribution of Bibles among the poor and the construction of new churches. He wrote voluminously on the Scriptures, producing commentaries and analyses of difficult Bible passages. He actually wrote more than a million words on theological topics, more than he wrote on science.

And like his predecessors, he believed his study of creation provided a window through which he could view creation. This was an extraordinary creation, one full of order and regularity, of pattern and design, of intelligence and purpose. For the first time in history, the phenomenal power of natural law was fully enunciated. And where did Newton think all this wondrous order had come from? At the end of the second edition of his seminal work *The Principia* he wrote: "This most beautiful system of the sun, planets, and comets, could only proceed from the counsel and dominion of an intelligent and powerful Being . . . This Being governs all things, not as the soul of the world, but as the Lord over all; and on account of his dominion he is wont to be called Lord God."[23]

But Newton's approach to his science was different from that of Copernicus three centuries earlier on the other side of the scientific revolution. Newton discovered the law that governed the motion of the celestial bodies—his famous law of universal gravitation. There had been no such concept of laws in

---

23. Isaac Newton, *Principia: the System of the World: Volume 2*, trans. Andrew Motte (Berkeley, Calif.: University of California Press, 1962), 669.

the cosmos up to this time. For Copernicus, God was directly and immediately responsible for the motion of the heavens, just as ballet dancers are directly responsible for whatever beauty might be a part of their performance. For Newton, God was the originator or source of the laws that governed the motion of the heavens. He was not the ballet dancer—He was the choreographer. Copernicus praised God as the producer of the motions; Newton praised God as the giver of the laws. God went from doer to designer.

This subtle shift in emphasis had far-reaching effects. God the Cosmic Designer was an entirely different being from God the Universal Agent. In the century following Newton, this new perspective was to lead to a drastically different interpretation of the relationship between science and religion.

Even though Newton himself remained committed to the Christian faith, his science contained some powerful seeds. When these seeds were planted and nurtured by scientists of different religious temperaments, they would grow into the hostility that eventually came to characterize the relationship between science and religion.

In Newton's universe, however, science and religion worked together. The order Newton described in his scientific masterpiece was clearly theistic in origin. But Newton was one of the last scientists who reserved a place for God in his description of the physical universe. Unfortunately, however, he did it by utilizing the God of the gaps hypothesis, an important element in the analysis that will follow and one that we examine briefly at this point.

The God of the Gaps

Contrary to popular impressions, Newton's universe did not run very smoothly. The planetary orbits had inexplicable wiggles in them, the moon did not move at exactly the right speed, and so on. It seemed Newton's remarkable scheme of explanation was just an *approximation* to what was going on in the universe. Left to its own devices, Newton's orderly universe would deteriorate to the point that it could hardly be described as orderly. Like a symmetrical lineup of runners losing its pattern as soon as the starting gun is fired, the pattern in Newton's universe should unravel. But the pattern was not unraveling. Why?

Newton formulated the first clear description of what has become known as the God of the gaps, or as Newton's particular application has become known, God must prod. Newton's theory of gravity, the theoretical foundation of the mechanical watchmaker universe, accounted for the gross details of the universe. The orbit of the earth around the sun could be roughly understood on the basis of the theory of gravity. But when you looked too closely, gravity didn't seem to be working correctly. So Newton argued that God must be periodically involved in the mechanics of the universe, correcting these little anomalies so that the order of the universe did not disintegrate into chaos. If Mars got going a little too fast, God would slow it down; if the moon got too close to the earth, God would pull it back out. Nothing would be allowed to get too far off course.

Newton's universe was like a dike with holes—unless somebody kept their fingers in those holes, all the water would eventually leak out. These holes, caused by small gaps in the theories, gave God something to do in the universe.

We now know that the dike has no holes. Newton's anomalies existed only in his data. They were all due to his incomplete knowledge of relevant details about the universe—things like the number of planets, the exact distance to the moon, and so on. One by one, God's fingers were removed from the cosmic dike, and no water came rushing through. It was eventually determined that the dike had no holes. So God had nothing to do.

Pierre-Simon de Laplace, with later and better information, plugged the holes in Newton's theory of gravity. He was able to show that the universe had no gaps, and many concluded that God, even if He existed, was not relevant to the cosmos.

A Theology of Holes

This God of the gaps theology was doomed to fail. It is not possible to develop an adequate description of God by simply assuming that He is responsible for whatever science cannot explain. Augustine's view that the whole universe was a theological object lesson was a better foundation for a meaningful theology of nature than the God of the gaps.

Unfortunately, the God of the gaps has proven to be a persistent, if not universally appreciated, partner in the dialogue between science and religion. Books are still being written by those who are convinced that something has finally been discovered that science will never be able to explain.[24] This curiosity becomes the basis for yet another God of the gaps argument, which is then promptly demolished by a new scientific discovery.

Gap theology has been in constant retreat for four centuries. But this is to be expected. The job of science is to close gaps in our understanding of nature. In fact, without gaps in our understanding of nature, there would be nothing for science to do. Once an adequate explanation is developed and all the gaps have been filled, science stops. As diligently as you may search for a lost coin, when it is found you stop looking.

A theology constructed from holes in scientific theories is like a pile of soap bubbles; as impressive as it may be at the moment, it will soon be nothing but a puddle of soap.

Summary

The position enunciated by Laplace was that there was no longer any need to invoke God as a part of a comprehensive scientific theory—a brash and arrogant position at the time. This is, however, essentially the position maintained by scientists today.

This is not, however—contrary to the expectations of some—an antireligious position. In fact, it represents the current perspective shared by most scientists, Christian as well as secular. It is based on the justifiable confidence that science has developed in its approach to the world. Science has indeed been

---

24. D. Lee Chestnut, *The Atom Speaks* (Grand Rapids: Eerdmans, 1951). For many years, one of the mysteries of physics related to the stability of the nucleus: How could all the protons, which repel each other, stay so tightly packed in the nucleus? Using a traditional God of the gaps approach, Chestnut argued that God must be the force in the nucleus. He based his theistic argument on the verse in Colossians, "By him all things consist" (1:17, KJV), which he felt should be literally translated as, "In Him all things hang together, or cohere." Chestnut suggested that this explanation should be called the "Colossian Effect." A few years after publication of *The Atom Speaks*, the actual physical mechanism for maintaining the stability of the nucleus was discovered.

successful in discovering scientific explanations for most natural phenomenon. That these explanations do not contain references to the Creator is no more an oversight than printed books failing to recognize the inventor of the printing press.

But when the scientific perspective is enlarged to include all of reality, the result is a one-dimensional worldview; in this case, the extreme position is that of naturalism. Naturalism assumes that all relevant information about the universe can be discovered by science, with the specific approach and methods of science. If science fails to find God in this search, then God must not exist.

It is folly to conclude that God does not exist because He cannot be discovered plugging holes in the cosmic dike. That is not the place to search for God. It may seem like a simpler approach, but it is doomed to futility before it begins. It is reminiscent of the man discovered on his hands and knees in the middle of the night searching for a lost wallet under a streetlight. When questioned, he confessed that he lost his wallet some distance from the streetlight but that he preferred to search for it where it was easier to see.

All that science has been able to do is demonstrate that God is not hiding in the cracks of the theories. He is not under the streetlight, as much as we might want Him to be there. That is not an appropriate place to search for the Creator of the universe.

A Look Ahead

Theology found itself challenged by the shrinking role God was playing in the physical universe. When the scientific revolution began, it was considered possible to prove the existence of God from science. When the revolution ended three centuries later, that same science was being used to disprove the existence of God. No wonder science was not universally embraced as an ally of the church!

In the next chapter we will analyze the separation of theology and science that emerged during this period and see how it has led to some of the problems we see today.

4

A Parting of the Ways

· · · · ·

*Science without religion is lame, religion
without science is blind.*

Albert Einstein

· · · · ·

Imaginary conversation in a monastery in Italy in the year
814—

Seeker: Father, how many teeth are there in the mouth of a
donkey?

Wise Man: That is a deep question, my son. The donkey is
the animal on which our Lord rode on His way into Jerusalem.
All the features of this animal therefore must be in perfect harmony with the larger truths of the Scriptures.

Seeker: Does Scripture tell us how many teeth are in the
mouth of a donkey?

Wise Man: Scripture does not say exactly, but we know the
number must make sense theologically.

Seeker: What difference could it possibly make to theology
how many teeth a donkey has?

Wise Man: All the details of the creation make sense, my
son; everything has a purpose and a place. God has given us
minds to discern these purposes.

Seeker: How might we discern these purposes?

Wise Man: Through contemplation.

Seeker: So if I sit silently and think carefully, God will reveal the answer to me?

Wise Man: If you meditate long enough, the pattern of creation will become clearer, and you will discover the right number of teeth for the donkey according to the eternal plan of God.

Ignorant Peasant: Why don't you just go outside and look inside the mouth of my donkey? It would be much quicker just to count the teeth than to talk about the "eternal plan of creation." Besides, I don't think my donkey is aware of any such plan.

Seeker: Tell me, wise man, should we go and count the teeth in the mouth of the donkey?

Wise Man: No, my son. That is not how Truth is discovered. God would not entrust the discovery of His eternal plan to our fallen senses.

Seeker: I will now retire to my chambers for the evening to think upon what you have taught me. I will pray that God will reveal this mystery to me.

Wise Man: Good night, my son.

Ignorant Peasant: Good grief!

Outline

This chapter, like the previous one, is historical. We will survey the same period of history looking again at some of the same figures but with a different point of view. The theme of this chapter is embodied in the famous quote from Albert Einstein: "Religion without science is blind." In the context of this chapter, the blindness to which Einstein refers is a metaphor for the state of religion in the absence of science. If science is not in dialogue with religion regarding the physical details of the universe, then religion does not have the tools necessary to find out much about that physical universe and will thus be poorly equipped to accomplish her tasks. Thus, we will see that those theologians who did their work without contribution from science came up with some very strange ideas about the nature of the physical universe.

When science and religion did enter into meaningful dialogue, the response of the Church was to embrace the new science, which was really just the old science of Aristotle, and elevate it to the level of dogma. This confidence turned out to be misplaced, however, and it was difficult for the Church to break its ties with Aristotle when his science was weighed in the balances and found wanting. The Church's strong reliance upon Aristotle as an authority in matters of science was one of the primary contributors to the conflict between Galileo and the Church, which is really the motivation for these historical discussions.

"Religion Without Science Is Blind"

Science as we know it today did not exist during the first 1,000 years of the Christian era. No one tried to argue that the natural world should be understood by simply observing it and that the mysterious laws governing the universe could be discovered through simple experimentation. Five hundred years before Christ, Aristotle had laid the foundations of what could have become science, but his approach had fallen out of favor. The philosophical foundations of the first millennium of the Christian era had been laid by Plato, the teacher of Aristotle, who approached the world of the senses from a dramatically different perspective. Plato had argued that the so-called real world was but a poor imitation of a more important world, that of ideas. All real world objects—the ships, shoes, and sealing wax of experience—were real only to the extent that they symbolized ideas. Ultimate reality was not located in these temporal objects, but rather in the world of ideas, which was accessible through the mind, rather than the senses. Platonic philosophy encouraged an approach to the world that was based on intuition or thinking, rather than observation.

Furthermore, Platonic philosophy considered the world of ideas to be much more important, much more real, than the world of things. If you wanted to study something important, you tried to make a connection with the world of ideas. You would not waste your time on the mundane superficiality that was available through the senses.

By emphasizing the authority of the mind over that of the senses, and insulting the world accessible through those senses, Platonic philosophy contributed to the establishment of a non-scientific perspective on the world. This perspective was then incorporated into the developing Christian tradition, which was already far more interested in the new heaven and the new earth than anything currently in existence.

By insisting that, loosely speaking, the mind was the authority in understanding reality, reality was forced to conform to patterns that made some sort of intuitive sense to the mind. If certain ideas seemed very appealing, then reality could be made to fit these patterns. Whatever might be concluded about reality by actually looking at it was not considered to be important. Thus, a fourth-century bishop could state that the structure of the heavens was modeled after the tabernacle of the Old Testament, even though there was no empirical evidence for that extraordinary construction.[1] The earth could be flat, the sky could be a firmament, stars could be hung out at night and then stored in a box during the day, and so on. If observation was not the authority in describing what was potentially observable, then there was really no need for explanations to agree with observations. Rather, the observations must be forced into agreement with the explanations. Square observational pegs were sanded down to fit into round conceptual holes.

But these observations were quite irrelevant anyway. No one was interested in the physical details of the earth; it was temporal, corrupt, and scheduled to be replaced shortly with a much better earth. What difference did it make if it was round or flat, stationary or moving, at the center of the universe or somewhere else? Figuring out the cosmos was a waste of time, like painting a house while it is on fire.

This perspective can be found in the writings of the leaders of the Early Church. One of these early theologians, Ambrose, who was a mentor of Augustine, wrote in the fourth century that "to discuss the nature and position of the earth does not help us in our hope of the life to come."[2] The scholars of this era were not, in general, against the study of the physical world per

---

1. J. L. E. Dreyer, *A History of Astronomy from Thales to Kepler* (New York: Dover Publications, 1953), 211. The bishop was Severianus, bishop of Gabula. His book was titled *Six Orations on the Creation of the World* and was accepted by many of the early Christian writers.

2. Ferris, *Coming of Age in the Milky Way*, 42.

se; rather they considered it to be an irrelevant and distracting pursuit that compromised one's focus on the spiritual life.

Ambrose's disciple, the great Augustine, shared the same perspective regarding the details of the physical universe and, while at some points in his writings he seems to be impressed with some of the more remarkable achievements of the Greek natural philosophers, he was convinced that these pursuits were of no ultimate value. Augustine was uneasy about the nature of the curiosity that drives people to search for the secrets hidden in nature. He argued that this curiosity was like a disease—one that could possess the mind and distract the attention from more important spiritual matters.

But the secrets of the universe during these unfortunate centuries were not the grand laws of physics that would be discovered during the Renaissance; Augustine might have approved of that enterprise. The curiosity to which he objects is the enthusiasm he saw in his contemporaries to find out about the more sordid side of nature, such as the freaks that were paraded in the local theaters.

Augustine sat on the intellectual summit of the first millennium. Christian theology was defined by his writings, and society as a whole gradually acquired his personal worldview, which, his followers assumed, included an aversion to studying the physical world. The following quote is taken from his masterpiece, *The Confessions*, one of the most influential books written in the first millennium. In this passage, notice the clear criticism of any learning that is motivated simply by curiosity or the desire to understand.

> At this point I mention another form of temptation more various and dangerous. For over and above that lust of the flesh . . . there can also be in the mind itself . . . a certain vain desire and curiosity . . . but curiosity for the sake of experiment can go after quite contrary things . . . through a mere itch to experience and find out . . . *Thus men proceed to investigate the phenomena of nature—the part of nature external to us—though the knowledge is of no value to them: for they wish to know simply for the sake of knowing . . .*[3]

---

3. Koestler, *Sleepwalkers*, 88, emphasis added. Koestler, like many modern historians of science, has lifted his quotes from Augustine in such a way as to make Augustine

Augustine goes on to warn against the dangers of suc-
cumbing to that sinful desire for knowledge. He states explicitly, "In this immense forest of snares and perils, I have cut off
and thrust from my heart many sins," one of which is the curiosity that makes men interested in natural phenomena, including "the course of the stars." The study of "the course of the
stars" at this point in time, however, was astrology. There was,
as yet, no distinction between astrology and astronomy, and it
was impossible to discourage one without the other.

Augustine is the most enlightened of the Early Church fathers. Both he and Ambrose still believed in the spherical earth
and were willing to look for alternate interpretations of biblical
passages that seemed to disagree with established notions
about the physical world. Lactantius, who lived in the century
before Augustine, had tried to pound the earth back into the
flattened disk that it had been thousands of years earlier. In arguments that would seem funny if they had not been widely
believed, Lactantius stated that people could not live on the
other side of the earth because they would fall off and that rain
could not fall on the other side of the earth because rain could
not fall upward.

Without exception, the thinkers who contributed to the formation of the Christian tradition shared this same attitude
about the scientific approach to the world. The focus of the first
10 centuries was so completely nonscientific that virtually no
progress was made in understanding any of the physical details
of the created universe, and a great many people were completely satisfied to believe that the earth was flat. By the time
the second millennium arrived, however, the round earth theory the Greeks had adopted 15 centuries earlier was just begin-

appear to be more antiscientific than is probably justified. Many of the criticisms that
Augustine levels at primitive scientific ideas are aimed not so much at the idea itself but
at the larger philosophical implications of the idea. When Augustine dismisses "Epicurus and his atoms" in *The City of God* (Book 8, Chap. 5) he does so in a paragraph followed by "The Epicureans . . . believed that life could be produced from lifeless matter,"
thus demonstrating that his concern was, at least partially, the larger philosophical perspective of the Epicureans, not just their views on atomism. In an era when science, philosophy, and theology were not recognized as distinct disciplines, scholars cannot be
criticized for their preoccupation with the apparent implications of scientific ideas.

ning to make its way back into Christian theology, like some sort of unwelcome prodigal son returning home after destroying the family name. But the prodigal had been gone a long time, long enough for the Church to have incorporated a very backward cosmology into the Christian faith.

This unfortunate state of affairs is all the more remarkable when considered in light of the intellectual brilliance of some of these early Christian thinkers. Augustine and his theological colleagues simply inherited, and then passed on, worldviews in which scientific progress was impossible. Augustine in particular should not be interpreted as the source of the long shadow that stretched across the Dark Ages as some contemporary historians of science would like to do; rather, he should be seen as a lonely light unable to dispel a very large darkness.

The end result of the nonscientific approach of the first few centuries was the medieval worldview, on which the imaginary conversation at the beginning of this chapter is based. In this conversation we sympathize with the unlearned peasant. It is common sense to look into the mouth of the donkey to count the teeth. Unfortunately, for the scholars of the medieval era, this kind of common sense was not all that common. Observation had not yet been recognized as a legitimate authority in the search for truth.

The medieval worldview, though, was the soil in which the seeds of science would eventually take root and grow. The lonely light of scholarship that Augustine had used to illuminate spiritual reality was still burning six centuries later when science arrived on the scene. This long tradition of scholarship, cultivated by the Church to learn spiritual truth, proved to be more than adequate to sustain the growth of the new science, which was about to leap from the 5th century before Christ into the 12th century after Christ.

The Rise and Fall and Rise of Greek Science

Even though the Greeks in the centuries before Christ had begun to develop a crude scientific perspective, this early progress was displaced by political upheavals and the growing influence of Christianity. The philosophy of Aristotle, who has been called the first scientist, contained the beginnings of science. If Aristotle's worldview had been allowed to mature, the scientific revolution might have occurred several centuries earlier. But Aristotle slowly faded from the canvas of Western civilization as the developing Christian worldview focused on Plato.

But even Plato lost his clarity as the Church fathers gradually subordinated all philosophy to their various interpretations of the Scriptures. The Greek "good old days" that were destined to be the motivation for the Renaissance had been almost completely covered over by the sands of time. Thus they lay dormant, waiting to be uncovered at some future date like a time capsule containing an antidote for the plague of intellectual malaise that gripped western Europe during the so-called Dark Ages.

Without even a primitive concept of science, the early theologians of the Church had been formulating descriptions of the physical world God had created. With their denial of the authority of observation, however, they were blind men describing scenery, deaf men describing sound. As a result, the 10 centuries passed with no progress in understanding the actual physical nature of the creation.

Thus, during the important formative years of the Christian tradition, theology stood alone. In a world of barbarians and disintegrating political structures it was the sole authority, fully responsible for the development of the Western worldview. This meant that no scientific limitations were placed on theologians to restrain speculative excess. The science that restrains responsible modern theologians from asserting nonsense about the physical world was not available to restrain the creativity of the Early Church fathers as they enunciated the first characteristically Christian theologies. They were free to start with the Scriptures and their traditions and build any kind of worldview that suited their particular philosophical disposition. They were free to make generalizations about the nature of the universe without fear of contradiction; humankind could be described in whatever terms seemed appropriate. As a result, a variety of extraordinary but absurd descriptions of the natural world, both physical and biological, crept into theology. These absurdities now stand as a testimony to the inadequacy of constructing a worldview without paying attention to the world that is being viewed.

It was acceptable, for example, to state that hell was located in the center of the earth, because there were no geologists to contradict that assertion. It was acceptable to state that the sinful Adamic nature was passed down through the seed of the father, because there were no biologists to say it couldn't happen that way. It was acceptable to state that the earth was flat, because there were no astronomers to say it was round. It was acceptable to say that the heavens were a tabernacle with waters suspended on top—and so on.

The freedom to make reality conform to preconceived patterns existed because there was no need for theologically based descriptions to agree with the observed properties of nature. Officially, there were no "observed properties of nature." Science was not yet trying to find out how the universe actually behaved. In fact, nobody was saying very much about the actual properties of the universe; it was a subordinate realm, not particularly important, and probably the abode of the devil. To make matters worse, most of the educated people who might actually have been able to learn something from nature were so preoccupied with spiritual exercises that the physical facts of the universe did not interest them.

Without empirical constraint, theology slowly painted itself into a dogmatic corner. By the time the Renaissance was beginning to feel the labor pains that heralded the birth of modern science, the Church had already developed a complete description of the universe, one that had been developed without ever actually looking at that universe.

The Opening of the Greek Time Capsule

Science arrived in the Western world at the end of the Dark Ages via cultural interaction with the Islamic world. Islamic scholarship had maintained a strong interest in the ideas of the Greeks and was conversant with the science of Aristotle. When this science wandered into the classrooms of the monasteries and began to expound on the *true* nature of the universe, the theologians sat up and paid attention. Who was this authority making controversial statements about the world that were at odds with the conventional wisdom? Who was this Aristotle that people were so enamored with his philosophy? Who would dare suggest that Aristotle had discovered anything important about the universe? Religion was the sole authority; it had been for more than 10 centuries. All truth was religious truth.

The protest from the religious establishment went unheeded. Intelligent people, still infected with the disease of curiosity that centuries of suppression had been unable to eradicate, were drawn to the philosophy of Aristotle. Here at last was a worldview that seemed to spring from within the human mind, one that answered the unasked questions that society had forgotten how to pose.

The popularity of Aristotle became a serious problem for the religious status quo. But there was probably no need for worry. Aristotle could be suppressed. So in 1210 in Paris, the Roman Catholic church issued the following decree: "Neither the books of Aristotle on natural philosophy nor their commentaries are to be read at Paris in public or secret, and this we forbid under the penalty of excommunication."[4]

For a while, as long as Aristotle was the "new kid on the block," the Church was successful in either ignoring or suppressing him. But the new kid became popular. People got very interested in this strange and wonderful new thing called science—and this science was making all kinds of statements that seemed quite relevant for theology.

Thus, in an effort to maintain its relevance in the face of the growing interest in science, theology was forced to address the issues raised by this new authority. But this new authority was not the modern authority we call science. The modern authority is based on the creative and dynamic synthesis of observation and explanation. While something like this had been the personal motivation for the science of Aristotle, it had certainly gotten lost in the medieval translation. In fact, by the time Aris-

---

4. E. Grant, *A Source Book in Medieval Science*, 3, in *Frame of the Universe*, Frank Durham and Robert D. Purrington (New York: Columbia University Press, 1983), 78. Originally published in L. Thorndike, *University Records and Life in the Middle Ages* (New York: Columbia University Press, 1944).

totle had marched across 15 long centuries from the open air of Athens to the dark classrooms of the medieval monasteries, he had aged considerably. Gone was the creative scientific approach to the problems of nature; in its place was another book to be placed on the pedestal of authority just below the Bible, to be consulted for final answers. By the time the science of the ancient Greeks arrived in the monasteries at the end of the Dark Ages, it had been transformed into something that fit naturally into the medieval worldview. It had become just another authoritative book.

The Father of Western Thought

Aristotle is considered by many to be the founder of the Western intellectual tradition, making significant contributions in many areas. A contemporary student of the liberal arts will encounter Aristotle in almost every course, whether it be philosophy, ethics, political science, astronomy, history, literature, rhetoric, or even biology. Many diverse areas of thought can trace an early form of their discipline to Aristotle.

When the Greek time capsule was opened, the ideas of Aristotle that had lain dormant for more than 1,000 years sprang forth and captured the stagnant imagination of the Dark Ages. Aristotle, it seemed, had explanations for everything: Why do things fall? Where are the stars? What are planets and how do they move? Why is the earth round? What is the best system of government? What is logic? How does one arrive at truth? What is the good life? Where did the universe come from? What makes a good poem?

The excitement generated by the philosophy of Aristotle gathered strength and blew across medieval Europe like a thunderstorm, rattling the shutters on monasteries everywhere. Scholars who had been walking for centuries with their hands folded and heads bowed were now forced to look up and behold the universe according to Aristotle. It was a remarkable universe, full of beauty and order, wonderful yet comprehensible, mysterious yet approachable. It didn't look at all like the one the Early Church theologians had described. If only Aristotle were not a pagan!

Because of Aristotle's pagan orientation, many of his explanations were at odds with the conventional thinking of the Church. But this pagan orientation seemed to provide no barrier to the popularity of his ideas, for Aristotle's thought stimulated something fundamental in human nature—the desire to satisfy one's curiosity. Aristotle was going to be a problem for the Church unless something was done, and banning his books just didn't seem to work. So the Church decided, "If you can't beat them, join them."

The job of reconciling Aristotle's thought with conventional church doctrine fell to Thomas Aquinas, the creator of the medieval synthesis, the basis of the strongest worldview in the Western tradition.

Two Authorities

In a remarkable achievement, whose details need not detain us, Aquinas merged the thought of Aristotle with the theology of the day. Arguing that reality needed more than one authority for a full description, Aquinas distinguished between revelation and reason or nature and grace. Theology was the authority in matters of revelation, and philosophy or reason—which came to include science—was the authority in matters relating to the natural world.

Aquinas described his synthetic worldview in his masterpiece *Summa Theologica*, written in the middle of the 13th century. Developing a comprehensive worldview that incorporated the best from all the relevant authorities, Aquinas argued that all truth was one; there should be no confrontation between science and religion, or reason and faith. Properly understood, these two great systems of thought complemented each other.

For Aquinas, science and religion were not irrelevant to one another. He argued that the physical structure of the universe described by Aristotle had theological meaning. The celestial bodies were round, for example, because that was a perfect shape, the kind of shape a perfect God would use. The earth was at the center of the universe because it was the home of humankind, the focus of the creation. The earthly realm was imperfect and changing because of sin. The heavens were perfect and unchanging because there was no sin there. Each element fit naturally into a larger, intellectually appealing pattern.

Aquinas attached a theological explanation to each element of Aristotle's description of the universe. Within the context of the medieval worldview, everything in nature discovered by science made sense in the context of theology. Science provided the facts about nature; theology provided the explanation.

Science and Theology as Partners

The medieval worldview of Aquinas was remarkable for a number of reasons. (1) There was no disagreement between the competing authorities of science and religion; each had an important role that complemented the other. (2) It dealt with all of reality, natural as well as spiritual. (3) It was so compelling in its logic and internal coherence that it commanded allegiance in a way that has never been duplicated since. Once understood, the grand system of Aquinas seemed obviously correct and completely impregnable.

Science and theology were so closely linked in the Thomistic worldview that it was impossible to tell where one stopped and the other began. A tradition of reading the Bible and finding science within its pages developed. Theologians were able to find proof texts for the shape, location, and immovability of the earth. In fact, it became difficult to determine whether the earth had the shape it did because science said so or because theology said so. This problem was also compounded by the fact that books were scarce in the centuries before the invention of the printing press.

Unfortunately, the scientific elements of the medieval worldview, which had been appropriated from Aristotle, were almost completely wrong. The earth was not perfectly round, it was not at the center of the universe, and it was not immovable. The sun was not a perfect sphere, without spot or blemish; the heavenly realm was really the same as the earthly realm, just farther away; the moon had irregularities; air did not fall up; and so on down the list. There were very few of the scientific elements of the medieval worldview that could withstand the scrutiny of observation. One by one, like dominos, these elements started to fall, tipped over by simple observations.

As we saw in the previous chapter, the Renaissance introduced many new scientific ideas. Theology found itself challenged by many of these developments. Biblical proof texts for discarded scientific ideas became an embarrassment to the Church. Statements made by respected church authorities were later recognized as absurd, creating credibility problems for those authorities. In fact, the whole issue of authority was becoming a thorn in the side of religion.

Having wedded its theology to some very particular scientific notions, namely those of Aristotle, the Church was in the uncomfortable position of having to modify its theology in response to purely scientific developments.

When Copernicus moved the earth from the center of the universe, theology had to adjust. When Kepler discovered that the planetary orbits were not perfectly circular, theology had to adjust. When Galileo showed that the sun and moon were not perfect spheres, theology had to adjust. When Newton unified the heavens and the earth with his theory of universal gravitation, theology had to adjust.

This constant need to modify its theology created a serious problem for the Church. How could the Church, as the recipient and guardian of God's eternal truth, be constantly in error? It is one thing to have a wrong idea; it is quite another to say that you got that wrong idea from God himself.

As civilization progressed from the stormy days of the Renaissance, many theologians became increasingly uncomfortable with science and began to lose interest in trying to integrate the two fields into one coherent whole as Aquinas had done earlier. The house of religion could not afford to have any of its foundations resting on the constantly changing soil of science. That rare breed of scholar capable of addressing the deeper questions of both disciplines approached extinction. Science was science, and theology was theology, and that was that.

Many argued that science and religion should part company. Reality was carved up, to be shared between the two authorities of science and religion. The science books were removed from the shelves of the theological libraries, and the dialogue between religion and science faded into a bad memory. Science would no longer have any authority in matters of religion as it had in the days when the Church would compromise in order to preserve the ideas of Aristotle. Religion would have no authority in matters of science as it did when the Church so vigorously opposed some of Galileo's discoveries. On controversies that lay within the demilitarized zone between science and religion, there would still be disagreement because no procedures had been developed to resolve such controversies. Religion became the sole responsibility of the theologians, just as it had been 1,000 years earlier before science started making so much trouble—only this time the theologians would carefully try to avoid making scientifically relevant statements.

The Contemporary Scene

The purpose of the previous discussion, which is far too brief to do justice to this complex subject, is to provide some background for an analysis of the contemporary scene. If we understand history, we can be more objective with the present, recognizing that the past exerts a great deal of influence on the present. We can perhaps recognize that even our own personal perspective is profoundly influenced by what has gone before. And we can try our hardest—Hegel notwithstanding—to "learn something from history."

Within the many strands of the Christian tradition, which comprises both Catholic and Protestant, liberal and conservative, are many different perspectives on this complex topic. The particular approach taken by a given person or group depends on the assumptions of their theology, which depends on where they are located within the Christian tradition. In reality, there is a characteristic worldview associated with many religious groups. This worldview will often determine the particular status of religious and scientific authority.

Ian Barbour, who has doctoral degrees in both physics and theology and has spent his life studying the interaction of science and religion, summarized the current status of this complex relationship in his 1989 Gifford Lectures. (The Gifford Lectures are an annual lecture series given by prominent scholars on the topic of natural theology, which frequently involves an integration of religion and science.) Barbour warns of the dangers associated with basing a worldview on a single authority. In this discussion, he contrasts the extreme scientific emphasis with the extreme fundamentalist position, which he calls biblical literalism:

> Scientific materialism is at the opposite end of the theological spectrum from biblical literalism. But they share several characteristics that lead me to discuss them together. Both believe that there are serious conflicts between contemporary science and classical religious beliefs. Both seek knowledge with a sure foundation—that of logic and sense data, in the one case, that of infallible scripture, in the other. They both claim that science and theology make rival literal statements about the same domain, the history of nature, so that one must choose between them.

> I will suggest that each represents a misuse of science. Both positions fail to observe the proper boundaries of science. The scientific materialist starts from science but ends making broad philosophical claims. The biblical literalist moves from theology to make claims about scientific matters. In both schools of thought, the differences between the two disciplines are not adequately respected.

> In a fight between a boa constrictor and a wart-hog, the victor, whichever it is, swallows the vanquished. In scientific materialism, science swallows religion. In biblical literalism, religion swallows science.[5]

A satisfactory contemporary worldview can only be developed somewhere in the middle of the spectrum bracketed by the extremes of scientific materialism and biblical literalism. Unfortunately, perfect clarity lies only at the extremes. If we venture into the middle of the broad spectrum, we find ourselves confronted with multiple authorities making conflicting claims.

---

5. Ian Barbour, *Religion in an Age of Science* (New York: Harper and Row, 1990), 4. Copyright © by Ian Barbour. Used with permission.

From this middle perspective both science and religion have authority, but it is hard to discern where one stops and the other begins. Religion recognizes that science has a legitimate claim to authority, but it is careful about letting the camel of science into the tent of theology. Science recognizes the validity of religious authority but is careful to keep that authority out of the laboratory. If science disagrees with the Bible, then an effort should be made at reconciliation. The nature of that reconciliation, however, might depend on whether the scientist or the theologian is doing the reconciling.

Summary

There are three important lessons to be learned from this chapter.

1. "Religion without science is blind." As we saw by considering some of the attitudes toward science expressed by the Early Church leaders during the first millennium of the Christian era, religion needs science to avoid the adoption of a worldview that is totally out of touch with the natural world.

2. There is no *normal* perspective that can be extracted from history to set up as a standard against which the claims of the modern antagonists can be measured. The relationship between science and religion has been in continual flux throughout time across the spectrum of the religious community.

3. The claim of the fundamentalists that the Bible can be an authority in matters of science is really nothing more than an attempt to revive the long discarded dogma—"nothing is to be accepted save on the authority of Scripture." This perspective was used to argue against a round earth, sunspots, moons around Jupiter, a moving earth, an infinite universe, and so on. Now this perspective is being used to argue against an old earth, an expanding universe, the big bang theory, continental drift, any form of biological evolution, and so on.

The perspective of the biblical literalists is a minority position. Nevertheless, it is a powerful one and, due to the silence that most theologians maintain on matters of science, it is often the only one that is heard in the evangelical community as eager ears listen for a voice telling them how to integrate modern science with their faith. A persuasive and eloquent argument can be heard that biblical literalism is the only possible foundation for a legitimate Christian worldview, that modern science must be rejected whenever it appears to disagree with a literal interpretation of the Bible, that science and religion must be enemies.

Fortunately there is a middle ground, a place to stand where both modern science and the faith of our fathers can be embraced. There is one God and one creation. The God of Abraham, Isaac, and Jacob is the same God that Einstein came to revere as he probed the deeper mysteries of the physical universe.[6]

Modern science is making great progress in understanding the universe that was created by God. And it is no accident that many scientists, like Einstein, are moved to reverence by their discoveries. It cannot be that this science that studies the creation knows nothing of the Creator.

---

6. We must, of course, distinguish between one's *experience* of God and one's *concept* of God. I believe that Einstein's reverential response to his work was due to the fact that the Creator is revealed in the architecture of His creation, and a scientist cannot spend too much time studying the creation until he or she experiences something of its Creator. Einstein rejected the God of traditional religion, and this restricted focus prevented him from developing an adequate concept of God (if one can speak of such a thing!). On the other hand, modern theologians, like Barth, who refuse to consider the revelation of God in nature, are also restricting their focus and, like Einstein, are missing an essential theological ingredient. It is one of the arguments of this book that God is profoundly beyond our grasp and we are thus restricted to "partial views." The more of these "partial views" we can assemble, the more adequate will be our theology.

5

Evolution: Biological Theory or "Long War Against God"?

• • • • •

In the beginning God created the heavens and the earth.

Gen. 1:1

• • • • •

John Washington Butler was a farmer from rural Tennessee. He taught school part time and was the clerk of the RoundLick Association of Primitive Baptists. Like all the fundamentalist Christians of his day, he believed in the literal truth of the Bible, and he was fed up with the educational system that was teaching the young people of Tennessee about Charles Darwin's theory of evolution, saying that "man has descended from a lower order of animals."

John Washington Butler was also a state representative in the Tennessee Legislature and in a good position to do something about this problem. So he wrote the following bill, which eventually became the law of the land in Tennessee: "That it shall be unlawful for any teacher in any of the Universities, Normals and other public schools of the State which are supported in whole or in part by the public school funds of the State, to teach any theory that denies the story of the Divine Creation of man as taught in the Bible, and to teach instead that man has descended from a lower order of animals."[1]

---

1. John T. Scopes and James Presley, *Center of the Storm* (New York: Holt Rinehart and Winston, 1967), 52.

On January 28, 1925, the bill passed by an overwhelming margin of 71 to 5. Six weeks later, the bill passed the senate by a margin of 24 to 6, and on March 21, 1925, Governor Austin Peay signed it. It was now illegal to teach Tennessee schoolchildren any theory of origins that differed from that described in Genesis.

The American Civil Liberties Union, self-appointed watchdog of the Constitution,[2] decided they didn't like the antievolution law Tennessee had passed. They felt it violated the constitutional separation of church and state by requiring the public schools to teach what they felt was essentially a religious doctrine. So about a month after the law went into effect, the group started running an advertisement in the *Chattanooga News*, trying to find a guinea pig who was willing to break the law of Tennessee by teaching the theory of evolution. They offered to pay the legal expenses of this criminal who, presumably in the name of open-mindedness or science or some such high calling, would confess to committing the crime of teaching evolution to Tennessee schoolchildren.

Everyone knew the proposed legal confrontation would be a big show, with big shots playing the major parts. Probably the famous William Jennings Bryan, three-time presidential candidate and one of the country's greatest orators, would defend the constitutionality of the law. And the ACLU would certainly recruit some big guns to fight on their side.

The Chamber of Commerce of tiny Dayton, Tenn., decided it would be good for business to have the big contest in their town. So they asked one of the few genuine liberals in the town, a local physical education teacher, if he would be willing to play the star role in the show they were putting together. The teacher was not sure that he had ever taught evolution, but he had filled in once for a biology teacher and had helped some stu-

---

2. It is very curious and worth noting that the ACLU recently defended a scientific creationist who was dismissed from the staff of *Scientific American* magazine for his views on origins. His creationism in no way interfered with the objective discharge of his responsibilities at the magazine, but he was let go simply because *Scientific American* did not want any of their readers to know they had a creationist on their staff. It is the opinion of the ACLU that *Scientific American* violated their former staff writer's constitutional right to believe as he saw fit. This incident helps put the ACLU in perspective. Politics makes strange bedfellows.

dents review from a textbook, *Civic Biology*, that did contain the theory of evolution. As it turned out, that was close enough—and John Scopes was arrested for teaching a theory of origins that was in disagreement with the literal teachings of the Book of Genesis.

John Scopes stood trial and was defended by the famous agnostic lawyer Clarence Darrow. As expected, William Jennings Bryan was the prosecuting attorney. The press descended on Dayton like flies on a piece of meat; all America was treated to a play-by-play description of one of the most famous intellectual contests in history. The *Courier Journal* of Louisville, Ky., ran a headline on July 21, 1925, which read "3,000 AT TRIAL, GET THRILL." The "Monkey Trial," as it became known, was billed as a really big show, and it did not disappoint. The prosecution won the case, although the verdict was not of particular interest (Darrow, the defense attorney, had even asked the jury, all of whom were farmers, to return a guilty verdict so he could appeal to a higher court.) Scopes, who sat silent for the entire show and was never even called to testify, was found guilty and fined $100.

Tiny Dayton had pulled itself by its bootstraps onto the pages of history. The famous Monkey Trial courtroom still draws tourists, and William Jennings Bryan College, established to "defend the faith" of its famous namesake, sits on a hill overlooking the tranquillity of a small Tennessee town that had enough excitement in 1925 to last it a lifetime.

Bryan College sent John Scopes a catalog every year for three decades but eventually gave up on him.

Outline

This chapter introduces scientific creationism by way of the famous Scopes trial. The next four chapters discuss this movement in some detail, examining both its scientific and its biblical dimensions. In this chapter we will argue that the scientific creationists represent a literal approach to the Scriptures that leads them to extreme conclusions not shared by many other Christians, regardless of their approaches to the Bible.

At the end of the chapter we will consider the antievolutionary philosophy of Henry Morris, the founder and leader of the modern scientific creationist movement, as described in his book *The Long War Against God*. We will argue that his thesis—evolution is the root of all evils, past and present—is based on an inadequate definition of evolution.

The Verdict

The jury of 12 farmers in the famous Monkey Trial returned a verdict for the prosecution. John Scopes was found guilty. By any legal standards the creationists won the case. But it was a Pyrrhic victory; the media made the creationists look like the primates that they insisted were not their ancestors. Clarence Darrow even put Bryan on the witness stand, where he carefully manipulated him with a series of irrelevant questions about the Bible: Was Jonah really swallowed by a whale? Did Joshua really make the sun stand still? Where did Cain get his wife? Was there really a worldwide flood? Was the earth created in 4004 B.C.?

Transcripts of the trial[3] show that Darrow was quite successful in posing scientifically unanswerable questions to the unprepared Bryan, who ended up embarrassing himself.

At one point in Darrow's rather lengthy and irrelevant interrogation of Bryan, he was interrupted and asked, "What is the purpose of this examination?" The responses to this question by Bryan and Darrow quite fairly represent what each side thought the prosecution was trying to accomplish:

> **Bryan:** The purpose is to cast ridicule on everybody who believes in the Bible, and I am perfectly willing that the world shall know that these gentlemen have no other purpose than ridiculing every Christian who believes in the Bible.

> **Darrow:** We have the purpose of preventing bigots and ignoramuses from controlling the education of the United States.[4]

William Jennings Bryan was neither a bigot nor an ignoramus. He was simply a fervently committed fundamentalist Christian who assumed that the Bible should be the authority

---

3. See Clarence Darrow, *Attorney for the Damned* (New York: Simon and Schuster, 1957).
4. Ibid., 217.

on all matters on which it speaks. Like the Church at the time of Galileo, he felt the truth of the Bible should not be compromised by scientific theories and was not comfortable with any nonliteralist approaches to the Scripture. The entire Scopes trial was motivated by that very confrontation: the literal truth of the Bible versus the theories of the scientific community. Unfortunately, Bryan had never considered many of the issues Darrow raised and thus was made to look foolish in the eyes of a world that was watching closely.

The Monkey Trial eventually ended. The circus that had come to town went home. The tranquillity that had temporarily taken leave of tiny Dayton returned. Bryan died a few days after the trial and was uncharitably eulogized by the ever-clever Darrow: "A man who for years had fought excessive drinking, now lies dead from indigestion caused by overeating."[5]

In a different world Bryan might have been a martyr and his cause might have been inspired to greater effort. But such was not to be the case. When Bryan was laid to rest, the creationist cause died with him. The defeat was extraordinary and spread throughout the country. In fact, the outcome was worse than a defeat; the publicity actually increased the popularity of the very theory of evolution that the trial was trying to suppress. "Where one person had been interested in evolution before the trial, scores were reading and inquiring at its close. Within a year the prohibitive bills which had been pending in other states were dropped and killed. Tennessee had been made to appear so ridiculous in the eyes of the nation that other states did not care to follow its lead."[6]

The creation/evolution controversy temporarily abated, as if everyone had decided to let the Scopes trial decide the question. Many Christians discovered ways to harmonize modern science with the Scriptures, and in so doing learned to live at peace with both their faith and their modern worldview. Those who clung to the literalist view of Scripture decided that maybe it would be more useful to focus one's energies on evangelism,

---

5. Ibid., 228.
6. Fay-Cooper Cole, "A Witness at the Scopes Trial," *Scientific American*, Jan. 1959, 130.

rather than difficult passages of Scripture whose exegesis seemed of dubious value. For a few short decades the scientific community resumed its position of authority in matters of science, freed from the need for its theories to compete with claims that the Bible contained a scientific account of creation.

The Modern Creationist Revival

One of the important creationist sources that William Jennings Bryan used in the development of his theory of origins was George McCready Price. Price was a Seventh-Day Adventist and self-taught geologist of sorts who wrote a college textbook called *The New Geology* (1923). This massive 726-page tome suggested that all of modern science was in error and needed to be reconstructed according to a new geological theory, which he called flood geology. This new theory stated that all of the surface features of the earth, from the rivers to the mountains to the rock formations to the fossils in those formations, were laid down by the flood of Noah. It was a full-scale assault on the science of its day, requiring that all of the disciplines, from paleontology to astrophysics, start over. Confident that his book contained the final word, Price announced in 1924, one year before the Scopes trial, that "evolution is dead . . . This volume is merely a sort of funeral oration. *Requiescat in pace.*"[7]

About four decades later, in 1961, a fundamentalist Southern Baptist named Henry Morris decided that Price's new geology needed a fresh treatment, one from a more mainstream theological perspective. Morris teamed up with a respected fundamentalist Baptist scholar from Dallas Theological Seminary named John Whitcomb, Jr., and produced *The Genesis Flood*, an updated version of McCready's *New Geology*.

The publication of this seminal work marks the beginning of the modern and current movement known as scientific creationism and has generated scores of books, much controversy, and even another Monkey Trial, which has become known as Scopes II.

---

7. Quoted in Martin Gardner, *Fads and Fallacies in the Name of Science* (New York: Dover Publications, 1957), 132.

The modern creationist movement is inspired by many of the same elements of the worldview that animated the Church fathers, the medieval church, and William Jennings Bryan: namely, that the Scriptures are the ultimate authority on all matters on which they speak, not just those related to religion. All the various authorities discussed in the first chapter of this book must be subordinated to the Scriptures, since they are the only source of absolute knowledge. Thus, when the Bible speaks of history, it is completely accurate in all details; it does not share the fate of other history books that generally have a few of their facts in error, due to the incomplete information of the author. When the Bible speaks of science it does so with complete accuracy; if the Bible appears to be in disagreement with contemporary science, then that science is wrong. In fact, scientific theories that disagree with the Bible are destined to be discarded and replaced with ones that will agree with the Bible.

Interpretation of Scripture

At the very heart of the scientific creationists' view of Scripture is the requirement that it be interpreted literally. Passages that are considered allegorical or historically conditioned by many biblical scholars are taken at face value by these fundamentalists.

This view of Scripture holds that the Bible is not limited in any way by the primitive worldview of the cultures in which it was written. The biblical writers were inspired by the Holy Spirit in such a way that their writings transcended their particular cultural circumstances. This transcendence allowed them to write statements about modern science that would have been incomprehensible to them. So even though the author and his culture might all believe that the earth was flat, when that author wrote inspired scripture, he would always write that the earth was round, *even though that would make no sense to him or his contemporary readers*. This creates the interesting paradox in which an inspired author produces scripture that would not be relevant to his own generation. It would only be a later, more scientifically advanced generation that would be able to comprehend those scientifically prophetic passages. It would even be conceivable that the Bible could anticipate new scientific discoveries. As Henry Morris wrote—

> The real truth of the matter is that the Bible indeed is verbally inspired and literally true throughout. Whenever it deals with scientific or historical matters of fact, it means exactly what it says and is completely accurate. When figures of speech are used, their meaning is always evident in context, just as in other books. There is no scientific fallacy in the Bible at all. "Science" is *knowledge*, and the Bible is a book of true and factual knowledge throughout, on every subject with which it deals. The Bible *is* a book of science![8]

The author goes on to enunciate a rather extensive list of modern scientific topics[9] he claims were actually anticipated by the Bible. This list includes such topics as Einstein's famous equivalence formula relating mass and energy, $E=mc^2$, which the above author claims can be discovered in Heb. 1:3 and Col. 1:17; radioactivity (2 Pet. 3:10); the circulation of blood (Lev. 17:11); Newton's theory of universal gravitation (Job 26:7); and radio waves (Job 38:35). These are a few concepts the author thinks he has discovered in the Scriptures. When these references are examined carefully, they do not support the claims made on their behalf. It would certainly be interesting if they did, but they do not.

The modern creationist movement is convinced that it has discovered the final answer to all questions relating to origins. They have discovered exactly what the biblical writers meant each time they made a reference to the natural world. They have shown that all apparent disagreements among the authors of Scripture are illusory, and they have demonstrated that all of modern science, from physics to hydrology, is founded on the Scriptures.

Furthermore, they have amassed a vast amount of scientific data that provides external vindication for their biblical cosmology. Fellow biblical literalists who hold alternate interpretations of Genesis are criticized for being deluded and for actually

---

8. Henry Morris, *Many Infallible Proofs* (San Diego: Creation-Life Publishers, 1974), 229.

9. Ibid., 242.

harming the cause of religion. Christians who refuse to make the Bible the final authority in matters of science are described as apostate, and actively working to damage religion. And anyone who does science without consulting the Bible is a secular humanist whose motivation can only be the destruction of religion, they contend.

Scientific Creationists Versus Other Biblical Literalists

The modern scientific creationists insist that the Bible is literally true in all its details. This mode of interpretation, biblical literalism, has had adherents ever since the Bible was written. But the biblical literalists have not always been able to agree on what the Bible is actually saying, even though they will take literally whatever they think it is saying. As we discussed in the first chapter, one's religious tradition plays an important role in how he or she interprets the Bible.

The scientific creationists, however, insist that there is only one possible interpretation of the biblical account of origins. Thus they quarrel, and not only with liberal "compromisers" who allow that the Bible might not be entirely accurate in all matters, especially matters of science. They also quarrel with other biblical literalists who, in spite of the fact that they share the creationist' high view of Scripture, simply have a different interpretation of the message of those scriptures.

For example, one long-standing point of disagreement among biblical scholars has been the meaning of the word "day" in Genesis. The first chapter of Genesis tells us that God created everything over the course of six apparently consecutive days, after which He rested for a seventh day. The most straightforward interpretation would suggest that these days are 24-hour periods—the same kind of days we have on our modern calendar. But for a variety of reasons, one of which is the somewhat different account in the second chapter of Genesis, many scholars have felt that "days" should have an alternate interpretation. One such alternate view is that the days were long periods, perhaps corresponding to geological epochs. This is sometimes called the day-age theory. Another view is that the days were ordinary days, but separated by long periods of time.

One very familiar interpretation is the gap theory, which suggests that there may have been a vast period of time between the first and second verses of Genesis. This vast period of time could accommodate many physical processes, including some form of animal evolution. Another very original interpretation suggests that the days were days of revelation, that is, that God communicated the story of creation to somebody, maybe Adam or Moses, over a period of six days.

Each of these different interpretations are legitimate attempts by biblical literalists either to fit the creation narrative into an acceptable modern framework or to reconcile the two different creation accounts. Each has a number of subscribers who faithfully insist that the Bible is absolutely *true* in all of its details, even though it might not be absolutely *clear* in all of those details, as evidenced by the divergent views.

But being biblical literalists is not enough for the scientific creationists: they insist that theirs is the only valid interpretation of these difficult biblical passages. They spend much effort, for example, trying to convince everyone that the only reasonable meaning for the days of Genesis is the modern concept of the 24-hour day. They view all alternate interpretations as compromise positions that impugn the integrity of the Bible by ascribing something other than the simplest of the various literal meanings to the first few verses of Genesis. It is acceptable for the Bible to use poetic language elsewhere, as it does when it calls God a Shepherd or Jesus a Lamb or Christians salt, but it is not acceptable to interpret the first few chapters of Genesis in this way.

The reason that the scientific creationists are so opposed to these various nonliteral or even alternative literal interpretations of Genesis is that all such interpretations make it possible to harmonize some aspects of modern science with the creation account. For example, if the days represent geological epochs, then it would be possible for some species to evolve during these long days and thus produce the apparent evolutionary sequence found in the fossil record. On the other hand, if the six days of creation are simply six days of revelation, then it would be possible to insert the entire evolutionary sequence into the

Genesis account. It would be possible to suppose that God had used evolution to accomplish some aspects of His creation and then simply told the original author of Genesis what He had done, after the fact, over the course of six days.

Nobody can put a final answer on these difficult questions relating to biblical interpretation. There are scholars with impeccable credentials and unassailable Christian character who hold widely divergent views. And there are many scholars comfortable with several of the various interpretations, convinced that the issue is of no relevance to the central message of the creation account. Thus, it is very hard to agree with the scientific creationists when they insist that it is of ultimate theological importance that Christians hold only their particular interpretation of the Genesis account.[10]

Tragically, this ongoing argument is between Christians who are in complete agreement on virtually everything. The scientific creationists are attacking their Christian brothers and sisters simply because they differ on minor points of interpretation of Genesis. There is no disagreement over such central doctrines as the Incarnation, the Virgin Birth, the Resurrection, heaven and hell, salvation, and the reality of miracles. But ploughshares are being beaten into swords so that a weapon will be available for an unholy war against another member of the Body of Christ. Magazines have sprung up, books are being written, tithe money is being diverted from traditional applications and being spent to finance efforts to show, for example, that the earth is young. Valuable energies are being squandered in the battle over biblical interpretation.

The victor in this foolish contest will get to decide what "day" means in Genesis, hardly compensation for the efforts of battle. But these scientific creationists still insist that "any interpretation of Genesis which accommodates the standard system of evolutionary geological ages is a clear-cut compromise with atheistic evolutionism, and it is very sad that Christians who

---

10. See, for example, Ken Ham, *The Lie: Evolution* (El Cajon, Calif.: Master Book Publishers, 1987), for an impassioned presentation of the theological necessity of a recent and literal six-day creation.

profess to believe the Bible as the Word of God will not acknowledge this."[11]

The scientific creationists have indicted many of the evangelical seminaries and colleges around the country because of their *error* on the meaning of "day." The Bible is being used as a weapon against a theory they are committed to opposing, no matter what other Bible interpreters or modern scientists may be saying about the matter.

Scientific Creationists Versus the "Nonconcordists"

Tied to the stake beside the compromisers indicted in the above quote are a group of Christians who fall into a group called nonconcordists. Nonconcordism is a school of biblical interpretation that starts with a different premise about the Bible than the scientific creationists. Nonconcordism assumes that the Bible is not a scientific document and thus should not be analyzed as if it were. To try to find science, modern or otherwise, in the Bible is thus a waste of time. It would be like trying to build an astronomical theory out of "Twinkle, Twinkle Little Star." Although this is a simplistic example, consider the folly of a literal interpretation of this rhyme, based on the assumption that it is a scientifically accurate account:

> *Twinkle, twinkle, little star.*
> *How I wonder what you are,*
> *Up above the world so high,*
> *Like a diamond in the sky.*

If a scholar somehow got the mistaken impression that this rhyme was a literal theory of astronomy, he would be faced with all kinds of perplexing problems. The stars are "above the world," rather than all around it. The stars are "like diamonds," so they must shine by reflected light rather than generating their own. The stars must twinkle. The stars are "in" the sky. The stars are "little," and so on. To dissect this rhyme in preparation for a scientific examination, its real life must first be extinguished. What will remain will be neither science nor poetry;

---

11. Henry Morris, *A History of Modern Creationism* (San Diego: Master Book Publishers, 1984), 329.

the science was never there, and the poetry was destroyed in the analysis.

It is very legitimate to inquire about the type of literature contained in the Bible. If you believe the Bible is a book of science, then you interpret it according to that assumption. If you believe the Bible is not scientific literature, then you do not presume to find science within its pages.

A nonconcordist does not try to fit modern science into the Genesis account of creation. A nonconcordist sees the Genesis creation account as a theological affirmation of early Hebrew faith in Yahweh as the sole Creator of the universe. The writer of Genesis was attempting to communicate a theological truth: "God is the Creator." He was not trying to give scientific information. The references to "days" are poetic and involve literary license as the writer is making the account full, rich, and resonant with current religious practices—much the same way as Jesus included extra information in His parables, information that was not meant to be taken literally. It is not necessary to argue that the characters in the parables of Jesus—the prodigal son, the 10 virgins, the shepherd with lost sheep, the debtor, the servants with the various talents—were actual people to get the point of those parables. The truth of the parables is not in the literal stories they contain.

Nonconcordism is not a new modern liberal way of looking at the Scripture. It is based on the recognition that the worldview of the biblical authors was not the same as our modern worldview. Our modern worldview prompts us to make literal statements; we are expected to speak literally, because that is how we will be interpreted. We believe truth is communicated in literal propositions. This was not true for the biblical writers. Their view of truth was different from ours and often expressed in metaphorical language. They distinguished between the "heart of the matter" and the body of additional information that surrounded that heart.

For example, in Hebrew writing the number 40 frequently means simply "many." So if the Israelites wander for a long time in the desert, then the sojourn might be described as 40 years, even though the exact number could have been 35, 40, or

51. In the modern world 40 means precisely "one more than 39"; it does not mean many. To be fair to the biblical authors, we must allow them to express themselves in their own idiomatic style. If we deny the biblical authors the right to express themselves in the language of their own worldview, then we extract them from history and make them mere automatons, clerical slaves recording accounts in a language they don't understand, to be deciphered by a more sophisticated future generation.

Augustine was a nonconcordist. He felt the references to "days" in Genesis were poetic imagery. He did not hold this position because he wanted to reconcile the biblical account of creation with evolution. He preceded modern evolutionary theory by over 1,000 years. Augustine was simply trying to understand the first chapter of Genesis as he believed the author intended it to be understood.

Nonconcordism is a popular and growing school of biblical interpretation in the evangelical church today, much to the dismay of the scientific creationists, who see it as serious compromise with atheistic modern science. But it is hard to see how an approach to the Scriptures that dates back to the Early Church is a compromise with anything modern.

Many Evangelicals are attracted to this perspective because of its value in presenting the gospel to a scientifically oriented society. The gospel of Jesus Christ must not be taken captive by any worldview, but if it is not burdened with excess baggage about the "age of the earth," the "fixity of species," and the "days of creation," then it appeals more readily to those who embrace a contemporary worldview. Evangelism is poorly served when it is identified with any scientific theory, for the gospel rests upon historical facts—the events of Christ's death and resurrection.

Scientific Creationists Versus the Rest of the World

The scientific creationists attack fellow biblical literalists because they might have an alternate interpretation of some verses in the Bible relating to origins. They attack nonconcordist fellow Christians who dare to suggest that the Bible is not a book of science. They attack presentations of the gospel that do not explicitly contain their particular explanation of creation. But their most violent attack is on the entire structure of modern society, particularly science, which they feel has become totally infused with the Satanic power of evolutionary thinking.

In a fascinating book, *The Long War Against God*,[12] the leading scientific creationist and founder of the contemporary movement attempts to fully analyze the impact and origin of the theory of evolution. This book is one of the best examples of a one-dimensional worldview that can be found anywhere. It is based on the simple premise that evolution is the cause of every single problem that has ever plagued the human race and that Satan is the source of evolutionary thinking. What could be simpler?

With Satan as its champion, it is clear that much evil can be produced in the name of evolution. And so it is. Political evils like Nazism, communism, fascism, imperialism, and militarism are all the direct result of evolutionary thinking. The discussion of Nazism is even titled "Hitler—Evolution in Full Flower." Moral problems like abortion, homosexuality, prostitution, drugs, and even cannibalism are all rooted in evolutionary theory. All of the world's great religions, except Judaism and Christianity, are evolutionary in origin and thus evil. The modern educational system is an abysmal failure because its architects were evolutionists. Chemistry, physics, biology, and geology are all unreliable because they subscribe to theories that are evolutionary in nature.

The obvious objection to this grand oversimplification is the simple observation that all these evils existed long before Charles Darwin published his *Origin of Species* in 1859. How could evolution be responsible for evils before that date? While there may be some truth to the argument that the Nazi abuse of the Jews was partially justified by appeal to evolutionary principles, anti-Semitism certainly goes back far beyond 20th-century Germany. How did evolution cause the Babylonians to mistreat the Jewish people?

---

12. Henry Morris, *The Long War Against God* (Grand Rapids: Baker Book House, 1989).

And what about abortion and homosexuality? They have existed for thousands of years. How could evolution be responsible for them?

Evolution Becomes Evolutionism

Charles Darwin's theory of evolution cannot support the weight of all the great evils attributed to it. After all, this theory is nothing but an explanation of how new species arise through natural selection. Briefly, all he claimed was the following: (1) Offspring are not perfect copies of their parents. Sometimes they differ in ways that make them more suited to survival. They might be faster, taller, smarter, or more resistant to serious diseases. (2) Not all offspring survive, however, due to challenges such as a limited food supply or predators. The ones that do survive are the most "fitted for survival"—the fastest, tallest, smartest, healthiest. Thus nature selects the better animals and preserves them so that they can have offspring of their own, offspring that will inherit some of their valuable survival skills. (3) Finally, this process of constant selection by nature can lead to the production of a new species over time through the accumulation of a large number of tiny improvements. Darwin's rather lengthy treatise was simply his analysis of the evidence for the theory outlined above. It is probably worth noting that Darwin maintained his belief in God throughout the writing of his controversial book, in which he even makes reference to the Creator.

It should be clear that such a modest biological theory cannot claim the vast territory over which it is said to rule. The domain of Darwinian evolution is actually quite small. So to preserve the "evolution as the root of all evils" thesis, the author of *The Long War Against God* greatly expands the meaning of evolution. He starts by replacing the word *evolution*, which is a rather narrowly defined biological term, with the word *evolutionism*, which is a complete worldview.

The worldview of evolutionism is one we have encountered in previous chapters. (The reader may want to reread the introduction to chapter 2 for an example of an evolutionist worldview.) Basically, evolutionism is the same philosophical system as scientific materialism: that is, the universe emerged without plan from preexisting "stuff." The universe evolved and eventually produced the earth. The earth evolved and eventually produced life. Life evolved and eventually produced human beings. The key feature of evolutionism in this context is the lack of any reference to a Creator. The whole process is without direction. There is no meaning to anything. Life is a crap game; we are just lucky numbers, overly impressed with our own good fortune at having shown up on the cosmic dice.

If we equate evolution with evolutionism and define evolutionism to be "any worldview that does not recognize God as the Creator," then perhaps we can blame all the evil in the world on evolution. But this is a logical trick, not an honest analysis. We might just as well define gravity as "that which offers explanations that contain no reference to God" and conclude that gravity is the cause of atheism!

The Long War Against God proceeds to dismiss Darwin as a mediocre scientist—an evaluation not shared by most historians of science—and nothing more than "the catalyst for a revival of ancient paganism."[13] The book makes it clear that Darwin could not have accomplished his scientific work without the help of Satan, who was really the guiding force in Darwin's endeavor— what we would call the principal investigator. In fact, Darwin's theories were really grand schemes of deception. He was not, for example, actually trying to explain the origin of the differences between birds, as he claimed. Rather, he was subtly trying to develop a scientific theory that would help to disprove the existence of God.

The Long War Against God makes it clear, though, that Darwin was not the founder of the evolutionist worldview. But where did this terrible idea come from—the idea that the universe could run without God? Like Sherlock Holmes putting together the pieces of a challenging puzzle, *The Long War Against God* traces the origins of this evil worldview back through history. Thomas Aquinas and Augustine are implicated in this mystery, but they are the channels through which the evil flowed, not the source. A Roman philosopher named Lucretius is indict-

---

13. Ibid., 151.

ed, then Plato and Aristotle, but they got the evil idea from Thales, the first Greek thinker on record. But evolutionism did not originate with Thales. Where *did* it originate?

To make a long story short, *The Long War Against God* traces the origin of the theory of evolution back to the tower of Babel, where Satan is claimed to have presented Nimrod with the terrible idea, many centuries before Christ. Thus, the evil idea was able to spread throughout the world when God dispersed the civilization that attempted to build a tower to the heavens. So Lucifer himself is the founder of evolutionary thinking. In fact, the reason he rebelled and had to be cast out of heaven was because he believed in evolution! "The very first evolutionist was not Charles Darwin or Lucretius or Thales or Nimrod, but Satan himself. He has not only deceived the whole world with the monstrous lie of evolution but has deceived himself most of all. He still thinks he can defeat God because, like modern 'scientific' evolutionists, he refuses to believe that God is really God."[14]

Conclusion

If the scientific creationists are correct, there can only be one course of action for the Christian. We must heed their call to beat our ploughshares into swords so that we can do battle with the enemy. If modern science is nothing more than a satanic delusion and a conspiracy of deception, then we must cast it all aside. And not merely biological evolution—geology must go because of its theories about the age and formation of the earth. Physics must go because of its theories about radioactive decay, the big bang, and the origin of the stars. Chemistry must go because of its satanic explanations about the origin of life from nonliving chemicals. The entire structure of modern science must be torn down because it is standing on an insecure foundation—evolutionism.

Once the cathedrals of science have been dismantled, they can be rebuilt using a new blueprint—the Bible. Geologists must now take care, however, lest they discover a way to date the earth that shows that it is billions of years old. But, of

---

14. Ibid., 260.

course, there is no need to worry about the age of the earth, because that can be determined from the Bible. Physicists must be careful not to discover that the universe is expanding or that certain atoms have built-in radioactive clocks. And chemists must be careful, lest they discover a mechanism by which chemicals might be able to organize themselves into a living organism.

What is the Christian to make of all this? Can the science that has cured polio, put a man on the moon, reduced infant mortality to less than 1 percent, unraveled the genetic code, discovered quarks, and developed laser surgery be discarded as so much satanic delusion? Can we really throw out all of modern science and start over? For that is exactly what it would take to rebuild the explanation of the universe according to the scientific creationists.

There is a historical lesson to be applied here. Four centuries ago all of these same arguments were hurled at the new astronomy: the earth does not move, the earth is the center of the universe, planets like Jupiter cannot have moons around them, comets cannot exist, supernovas cannot occur. This was a biblically based science, a medieval scientific creationism challenging Galileo and accusing him of trying to undermine the biblical worldview.

But Galileo knew he was right. "The Bible teaches us how to go to heaven, not how the heavens go" was his defense against a religious inquisition. His pithy quote in the context of the 20th-century conflict would become "The Bible tells us who created the universe, not how it was created."

Several centuries later it is profoundly clear that Galileo was right. The Bible does not tell us how the heavens go. Now it seems we are being asked to climb onto the horse of progress and ride backward into the past, to a time before this lesson was so abundantly clear, to a time when the Bible was a sourcebook for science. But can we really do this with confidence? How can we be sure that history is not repeating itself? How can we avoid hindering the gospel of Jesus Christ by attaching it to some totally incredible explanation of the universe?

6

The Crime Against Galileo

• • • • •

The doctrine attributed to Copernicus, that the earth moves around the sun . . . is contrary to Holy Scriptures and therefore cannot be defended or held.

Cardinal Bellarmine

• • • • •

In 1163 at the Council of Tours, Pope Alexander III decided that it should be the task of the clergy to search out heretics. The recommended procedure was known as an inquest, in which witnesses would submit suspicions of heresy to an inquisitorial board who would then investigate the implicated heretics. The heretics under investigation would not be informed about the specifics of the suspicion, nor would they know the identity of their accusers. If convicted, the heretics could be excommunicated, which would mean, among other things, that they would go to hell when they died. The threat of excommunication was usually sufficient to persuade the most convinced heretic to change his mind. Some heretics still refused to recant, however, so about a century later, Pope Innocent IV, clearly misnamed, authorized the use of torture in the process of interrogation to help with the persuasion.

In 1592 the now-experienced Inquisition put a renegade Dominican monk named Giordano Bruno in prison for heresy. Bruno had dared believe in Copernicus' new astronomy and had even speculated that the universe might be infinite, filled with many worlds populated by diverse peoples. After eight years of imprisoning Bruno, the Inquisition tied him to a stake at Campo del Fiori and burned him alive. His ashes and his boldness were scattered to the four winds.

On October 1, 1632, a third of a century after Bruno met his untimely death, another old man received a summons to appear before what had by then become the most frightening examining committee in human history—the Inquisition of the Roman Catholic church. The old man under summons was crippled with arthritis and had developed a serious double hernia condition, which required him to wear an iron truss much of the time.

The timing was ominous. The Black Plague was spinning its evil web across Italy, gathering almost half of the population into its fatal snare. The historically omnipotent Roman Catholic church was watching the termites of reformation nibble at its foundations. Rome had been sacked a century earlier, and Spain had taken control of much of the Italian peninsula. Politics seemed unable to solve the domestic crises, and people were looking for figures of authority in whom to trust. The untimely summons would require a difficult journey of 200 miles, for winter lay deep on the countryside. Medical authorities pleaded with the church to leave the old man alone, but they were not to be dissuaded.

So, on January 23, 1633, the old man set out for Rome to appear before the Inquisition on charges of heresy. Unlike Bruno, the old man was not a professional theologian. He was just a scientist, and his heresy was purely scientific. He was accused of holding the opinion that the sun is the center of the world and immovable and that the earth moves.

The old man was Galileo Galilei, and the trial stands as the focal point of the historical conflict between science and religion.

Outline

This chapter introduces the Galileo affair in some detail. In preparation for the analysis of scientific creationism, which we will argue is analogous in many ways to the former anti-Galileo movement, we will be considering the theological, biblical, and scientific dimensions of the Galileo affair. We will see how

Galileo's antagonists argued that the radical Copernican hypothesis was unscriptural, unscientific, and impossible to reconcile with Christian theology. We will then see in subsequent chapters that these are exactly the arguments now being used by the scientific creationists to attack the modern theory of evolution.

History Repeats

There is a remarkable similarity between the Galileo affair and its modern equivalent—the antievolution movement. There is thus a valuable lesson to be learned by studying the Galileo affair, one that aids immensely in dealing with its contemporary reincarnation.

The story of Galileo is like a gem with many facets, each of which yields a different perspective on the gem, yet none of which can be said to provide a complete picture. Each of the various facets has its own cast of characters, its own heroes and villains, and its own lessons to be learned. Just when it seems Galileo looks most like a persecuted scientific martyr, victimized by a closed-minded and power-hungry church, the light of history will catch another facet of the gem and Galileo will look like an arrogant, cantankerous, self-serving social climber. When the light shifts again, the church will appear as an unwitting third party in the dispute, drawn into an irrelevant scientific argument.

In this chapter we will be considering some of the facets of the Galileo incident, ever mindful that there are other facets with their own and different stories to tell. In particular we will examine the very specific conflict between the literal truth of the Bible and a particular scientific theory. The scientific theory was that of Copernicus, the Polish priest/mathematician who suggested that the earth was moving about the sun and thus was not located at the center of the universe.

Copernicus' new astronomy grew out of the difficulties he had encountered in explaining the paths of the planets from the perspective of a stationary earth located at the center of the universe. Copernicus found that it made more sense to account for the observations by assuming that the earth went around the sun, and not vice versa. Copernicus knew, however, that his ideas would be difficult to reconcile with the teachings of the Church. He was right, and his ideas were eventually challenged on both biblical and theological grounds.

The Biblical Challenge to Copernican Astronomy

Some of the opposition to Copernicus came from those who read the Bible in a certain very literalistic way and felt his cosmology was incompatible with the Scriptures. Adherents to this extreme literalist position pointed out that Joshua commanded the sun, and not the earth, to stand still. The Psalmist declared that the earth "is firmly established; it cannot be moved" (Ps. 93:1); the sun is described as running: "Its rising is from the end of the heavens, and its circuit to the end of them" (19:6, RSV). The Bible seemed to be quite clear about both the position and the immovability if the earth.

If modern readers could somehow read the Scriptures without the powerful influence of recent tradition, they would probably also conclude that the Bible teaches that the earth is stationary. But we no longer believe that the earth is stationary, and those biblical passages that seem to claim otherwise have been reinterpreted over the years.

We should not be surprised to discover, however, that the Bible claims that the earth is stationary. After all, every one of the biblical writers lived at a time when a stationary earth was the prevailing view. If the inspired authors of Scripture had written that the earth was moving around the sun, their writings would have been dismissed by their contemporaries as nonsense, not preserved as valuable sources for theology.

Modern biblical literalists insist that the Bible does not teach that the earth is stationary. They claim that the biblical scholars who challenged Galileo and Copernicus were incompetent and incapable of interpreting the Bible properly. If they had been smarter, they would not have imputed such falsehood to the inspired Scriptures. But this list of incompetent biblical scholars includes some very important figures. In addition to the Roman Catholic scholars, who included Cardinal Bellarmine—"one of the greatest theologians the world has known"[1]—Martin Luther, John Calvin, and many of the key figures in the Protestant Reformation fall under the cloud of this indictment.

The obvious question arises: Why were *all* biblical scholars convinced that the Bible taught that the earth was stationary until such time as science clearly demonstrated that this could not possibly be true? Why was it so easy for them to read the Bible and discover an earth-centered universe within its inspired pages? And why is it that no modern biblical literalist can find *any* of these biblical arguments that were so convincing to their medieval counterparts? What is it about the modern approach to the Scriptures that finds them saying something different than they did in the Middle Ages? Can it be that even biblical literalists are so influenced by their worldview that they read the Bible in such a way as to provide confirmation for that worldview?

The medieval theologians were not incompetent; they were honest biblical scholars who failed to understand the influence that their worldview exerted on their interpretation of Scripture. Similarly, the modern fundamentalists are not incompetent. But they also fail to recognize that they are bending the Scriptures to support their worldview. Each of us wants to believe that all the authorities we trust agree with one another. We trust the Bible; we trust science. Surely they must, therefore, be in agreement.

The Theological Challenge to Copernican Astronomy

In addition to the biblical challenge, there was also a significant theological challenge. Copernican astronomy must be rejected because it undermines the very foundations of religion itself.

> It upsets the whole basis of theology. If the earth is a planet, and only one among several planets, it cannot be that any such great things have been done specially for it as the Christian doctrine teaches. If there are other planets, since God makes nothing in vain, they must be in-

---

1. Andrew Dickson White, *A History of the Warfare of Science with Theology in Christendom* (New York: Free Press, 1965), 129.

habited; but how can their inhabitants be descended from Adam? How can they trace back their origin to Noah's Ark? How can they have been redeemed by the Savior?[2]

This argument seems foolish today. But the words in the Bible have not changed—only the worldview of the readers of those words.

The Triangle of Conflict

The religious challenge to the new astronomy was not immediate. In fact, the first challenge came from the academic status quo, which we would call the scientific community. The church even went along with the new astronomy for a while but eventually was forced to take sides.

The Galileo affair must be understood as the complex interaction of three separate authorities: (1) the church, (2) the new "science," and (3) the medieval worldview, which the educational establishment accepted as absolutely correct.

1. The church was the Roman Catholic church, which had assumed almost full control over the intellectual climate of the day. The great schools in Italy were populated with priests, and even much of *secular* science was being done by scholars directly affiliated with one of the orders of the Roman Catholic church. Significant departures from church teaching were, in principle, punishable by death, but some flexibility was allowed in matters considered to be peripheral, such as esoteric questions of science and mathematics.

2. The new science was Copernicanism, specifically the idea that the sun and not the earth was the center of the universe. Copernican astronomy was well known at the time of Galileo but was widely interpreted as just a *model*[3] of the universe rather than an actual description of physical reality. Its popularity stemmed from the simplicity it lent to astronomical calculations. Calendar-makers, for example, found it much simpler to construct long-range calendars by assuming that the

---

2. Ibid., 130.

3. A well-meaning associate of Copernicus had added a preface to his book that proposed that the new theory should not be interpreted as description of physical reality, but rather just as a model.

earth was moving around the sun, rather than vice versa. Very few people actually believed, however, that the earth was moving through space.

3. The medieval worldview was the grand synthesis of Aristotle and Christianity that Thomas Aquinas had achieved in the 13th century. It was a comprehensive description of all reality, a genuine metaphysics that was accepted as practically self-evident by the academic community. Discussed at some length in chapter 4, to which the reader is referred for a more complete description, the key feature of the medieval worldview in this context is the elaborate interconnections that existed between its various elements. Each idea fit so snugly into the overall mosaic that the whole program would crumble if any individual idea were to be extracted. It would be impossible to deny the immovability of the earth, the existence of angels, the planetary spheres, or the immutability of the heavens without bringing the whole metaphysical house crashing down around one's ears. Thus it was that a criticism of certain esoteric notions of astronomy came to be construed as an attack on the theology of the Roman Catholic church.

These three authorities—the church, the medieval worldview, and the new science—were engaged in an uneasy competition to see who should preside over the questions raised by the new Copernican astronomy.

Galileo was a fully committed Copernican. He had subscribed to the new astronomy in his youth and did not consider it to be a mere model, a useful fiction. Copernicus was absolutely correct, argued Galileo, and he proceeded to develop a strong scientific case for his position. Before the Copernican astronomy could be established, however, it was essential to tear down the old Aristotelian edifice. The medieval worldview had to be dismantled to make room for Galileo's new program.

Galileo began by attacking the obvious problems with the physical science of the day, all of which was taken directly from Aristotle. Galileo showed that Aristotle was wrong about the causes of motion, the descriptions of floating bodies, the immutability of the heavens, and so on. Galileo's attacks were frequently personal, making fun of the professors at the universities as they tried to understand the world at the end of their noses while their noses were buried in books that had been written centuries earlier. On one occasion he wrote a satirical poem in which he referred to his university colleagues as little wax Aristotles, making light of their unquestioning acceptance of all things Aristotelian.

Galileo achieved considerable success with his new scientific approach. He successfully challenged much of the science of the day and managed to introduce many new ideas into science through his discoveries, both in the laboratory and with his new telescope. He became a widely celebrated author, read all over Europe and even in the Orient. The telescope brought him considerable fame, and he made a number of important discoveries, including the moons of Jupiter, sunspots, mountains on the moon, and so on. In subtle ways, though, his discoveries were poking holes in the seamless Aristotelian cloth stretched so comfortably across the Renaissance universe.

Aristotle had said everything must revolve around the earth. So how could there be moons around Jupiter? Aristotle had said the celestial bodies were perfect and smooth. How could they have mountains or spots on them? Aristotle had said that the earth was the center of the universe. How could it be revolving around the sun? In fact, on this last question there were even a number of biblical references that could be quoted in support of Aristotle, thus showing how the science and theology of the day were so thoroughly complementary.

Many of the discoveries of Galileo, such as the moons of Jupiter, were accessible to anyone—anyone, that is, who would look through a telescope. Amazingly, there were a number of Galileo's contemporaries—the wax Aristotles—who refused to look though his "devil instrument" lest they fall under the same heretical delusions that plagued Galileo.

The Church, appropriately more concerned with matters spiritual rather than scientific, went along with Galileo at first. In fact, he successfully converted many of the Jesuit astronomers at the Holy Roman College to the new astronomy, even though it required some adjustments in their scriptural exegesis. The wax Aristotles, however, marching in mental lockstep with a man who had been dead for 2,000 years, were not to be persuaded. Galileo was humiliating them at every turn, clearly showing that the material they were teaching in their classes was totally wrong. And Galileo's classes, like his fame, were growing in size while theirs were shrinking. It became clear that the comfortable worldview that had provided intellectual security for several centuries was about to topple, as Galileo slowly, and with much fanfare, removed it supports.

The Intrigue

The new astronomy was not going to disappear. Galileo was going to build the new universe, and the academic status quo was going to be very unhappy in that new universe. So they conspired to stop Galileo, hoping also to stop the spread of the ideas that were sprouting up in whatever soil he turned with his new scientific spade. Their strategy was to make the medieval cosmology a matter of faith. They knew people were much less likely to accept a new scientific idea if it contradicted their faith.

It was well known that the Copernican astronomy, if taken literally, was difficult to reconcile with the Bible, even though many of the theologians had expressed a willingness to confront that thorny problem in the event that the Copernican hypothesis could be demonstrated. Galileo's challengers decided that the Church needed to understand just how difficult it would be to reconcile the new astronomy with the old theology. So they convinced the Church that the new astronomy was *absolutely incompatible* with the Christian faith. They forced the Church to take a definite stand on the biblical references to the stationary earth, even though the Church was trying to keep the question open, since they knew that it didn't really matter all that much. However, the Psalmist had writen, "The world is firmly established; it cannot be moved" (Ps. 93:1), clearly contradicting any crazy notion that the earth might be rushing around the sun at thousands of miles per hour.

To make a long and fascinating story short, the Church was persuaded to investigate the matter officially. Cardinal Robert

Bellarmine, who held the pompous title of "Master of Controversial Questions," was appointed to study the problem.

Bellarmine was initially open. Although he did not accept Copernicus' theory, he indicated a willingness to consider it, even though he knew it would require a reexamination of some difficult passages in the Bible. But the wax Aristotles soon closed his mind for him. They pointed out that the new astronomy had difficulties that had not yet been worked out, so it seemed there were some scientific problems to go along with the theological ones. Galileo couldn't prove the Copernican theory to be correct, so there was really no reason to abandon good old Aristotle after all these years. Besides, many of the experts in the universities were condemning the theory of Copernicus; the Church might as well join them.

So the Church made a terrible mistake. They officially adopted the Aristotelian description of the universe as the only one that was compatible with their Christian faith. They condemned the theories of Copernicus, put his book on the Index, and made it formally heretical to believe that the earth goes around the sun. Believing this monstrous lie was now sufficient grounds for being burned at the stake. To be a Copernican was to be a heretic, to risk excommunication from the Church, to burn at the stake, and then eternally in hell in that special place reserved for the destroyers of the faith. The wax Aristotles had saved their medieval worldview for the time being.

But Galileo was right. In time everyone, even the Church, conceded this fact. And there are now billions of Copernican heretics on planet earth, all quite comfortable with the notion that the earth is going around the sun.

The Verdict

The Inquisition of 1633 forced Galileo to recant. But that verdict, like the one in the Scopes trial, is of little interest. It has even been officially rescinded by the Roman Catholic church. History has reached a far more significant verdict in its judgment of the Church. The deliberations are completed, the verdict is in, and the Church has been found guilty:

1. *guilty* of compromising the integrity of the Bible by insisting that it said things that turned out to be false
2. *guilty* of enhancing the credibility of science at the expense of religion, since that science was unambiguously vindicated by subsequent history
3. *guilty* of forcing thinking people to regard the teachings of the Church as antiquated, irrelevant, and unreliable
4. *guilty* of initiating the divorce of science from religion and making it appear that one must choose between them

The Galileo affair is officially over. But all of the questions remain as the same basic conflict between competing authorities is being revived in the current quarrel involving the scientific creationists. Before we look at its contemporary reincarnation, it will be helpful to summarize the essentials of the Galileo affair.[4]

1. The Church adopted the erroneous position that the Bible taught a specific scientific theory. Even though there were only a few isolated proof texts to support the dogma of the stationary earth, these were presented as proof that the Holy Scriptures taught that the earth did not move.

2. A scientific theory emerged that contradicted this specific interpretation of Scripture. This theory, that the earth goes around the sun and not vice versa, in reality had a very small impact on the theology of the day and is now considered to be theologically irrelevant.

3. Opponents of the theory, intellectually wedded to the old worldview and afraid to see its authority undermined, condemned the theory. To promote their condemnation, they greatly exaggerated the incompatibility of the new science and the old theology.

---

4. This summary is a gross oversimplification of a constellation of very complex historical events. Scholars are still fascinated with the Galileo affair, and new information is still being discovered, which forces reexamination of the basic issues. A recent contribution to the discussion is the book *Galileo: Heretic* by Pietro Redondi, which suggests that Galileo's views on the atomistic structure of matter were at the heart of the conflict and the charges of Copernican heresy were just a smoke screen. For our purposes here, I have distilled one aspect of the controversy because of its valuable lesson. The interested reader is referred to the vast literature on Galileo for more details.

4. Specific scientific problems with the new theory were magnified to suggest that the new theory was scientifically unsound, in addition to being heretical.

5. A false dichotomy was set up between the new theory and the faith, forcing people to make a choice, even though there was no need for such a resolution. The new theory became clearly recognized as incompatible with Christian faith. It was clear that the faithful must choose between the two; there could be no middle ground, no compromise.

The schism that emerged out of the Galileo affair has never completely healed. In Italy, where the incident occurred, science never resumed its role of world leadership. Italian science withdrew into an unproductive corner, hiding lest it inadvertently find itself on the wrong side of the heretical fence. The scientific revolution moved to England, where a more open theology ruled. The Church became polarized into two camps: those that accepted the tainted new science with its suspicions of heresy, and those who clung to the medieval worldview. These faithful few, who refused to compromise, became increasingly more out of touch with the culture in which they resided. Like exhibits in a museum, they became more remarkable as time went on; the world around them changed, but they stayed the same.

Once Again: A Worldview Under Attack

Like Galileo's century, ours has been one of frightening change. When the 20th century opened, there was a comfortable worldview in place. Inspired by the "law and order" universe of Newton, this worldview provided a constancy, a sense of the absolute. It had succeeded to some degree in emulating the medieval worldview as a self-evident theoretical system that was vindicated by common sense.

This century began with the discovery of quantum mechanics that demonstrated that the universe was not law and order but rather indeterminacy and uncertainty. The uncertain child conceived by the physicists was adopted by those looking for support for an argument that all knowledge was uncertain. The inherent uncertainty of knowledge, they argued, meant that there could be no absolutes.

Pouring salt into a new wound, Albert Einstein presented his theory of relativity shortly after the advent of the quantum theory. Once again the offspring of science was adopted by those who wanted to argue that everything, not just the space and time of Einstein, was relative. Truth was relative, morals were relative, religion was relative, they claimed, much to Einstein's dismay, as his theory was exploited by those who had no idea what it was.[5]

Relativity and uncertainty were not welcome guests in the house of Newton. Together with Darwin's theory of evolution, they ran about like disobedient children, knocking everything out of place and utterly destroying whatever sense of order had been achieved in the previous centuries. A powerful challenge was being laid before the Newtonian worldview, one that could not be ignored.[6]

The past few decades have witnessed the gradual adoption of the new worldview[7] as the old one has been weighed many times in the balances and always found to be wanting. But there has been widespread resistance to the new intellectual order on a number of fronts.

Just as the wax Aristotles of the 17th century resisted the Copernican challenge, so the scientific creationists are resisting

---

5. Einstein was dismayed by those who latched on to the word *relativity* in his theory and used it to argue that anything other than certain esoteric physical quantities was relative. So abused was this aspect of his theory that Einstein later wished he had named it "The Theory of Invariance," which would have been totally appropriate, given that the theory shows that the laws of physics are invariant in different reference frames. (See Nathan Rotenstreich, "Relativity and Relativism," in *Albert Einstein: Historical and Cultural Perspectives*, ed. Gerald Holton and Yehuda Elkans [Princeton, N.J.: Princeton University Press, 1982].)

6. In *The Closing of the American Mind* (New York: Simon and Schuster, 1987), professor Allan Bloom argues that "almost every student entering the university believes, or says he believes, that truth is relative" (25). Bloom's large book is a far-reaching analysis of this unfortunate state of affairs. While the physical theories developed at the beginning of this century should have made negligible contribution to this situation, the fact is that they were perceived by some as providing important scientific support for larger philosophical movements toward relativism.

7. As we argued in chapter 1, there are many diverse elements contributing to the contemporary worldview. This discussion is not meant to imply that the modern worldview, or any worldview for that matter, is solely (or even primarily) the result of scientific developments. But the scientific creationists are arguing that the theory of evolution is adequate to explain the origin of all of the problems of the modern world. Their assumption is that if we could get the right science in place, the rest would follow.

the contemporary challenge to their worldview, which is essentially Newtonian. And the strategy is exactly the same: (1) Convince the faithful that the new science is incompatible with the Bible; (2) magnify any problems with the new theories to make them seem unscientific; (3) force people to reject the new science before it matures to the point at which it cannot be refuted.

The Return of the Wax Aristotles

The wax Aristotles have been reincarnated as the scientific creationists who are once again attacking the science of the day. Quantum theory, astrophysics, geology, paleontology, zoology, genetics, relativity, and cosmology are all under fire because they are the foot soldiers in the war of the worldviews. Galileo has been reincarnated as Charles Darwin, who is the focus of the attack, although the attack is much broader than simply the theory of evolution.

The scientific creationists are using the same strategy employed by the wax Aristotles 300 years ago: They are attempting to convince the Church that their faith demands the rejection of all forms of evolutionary thinking, whether biological, geological, or cosmological.

The same triangle of conflict can again be discerned beneath the rhetorical fog that envelops this controversial subject. Just as Copernicanism was not immediately attacked as heretical, so modern science has had a brief honeymoon with the religious community. And most of Christendom has accepted the results of modern science and simply reworked its theology and biblical exegesis to incorporate the new ideas.

But there is a small group of very vocal Christians who are not willing to let go of the old worldview to make room for the new. They are attempting to marry the Christian faith to the old worldview so that one cannot depart without the other. The modern creationist movement has considerable grass roots support from some conservative Christians, but very little of this support comes from *scientists.*

So the question from the beginning of this book reappears: Who is the *authority* in matters of science? Is the Bible the final authority? Should we interpret the Bible literally and force our scientific theories to conform to that authority? Or should we allow science to be the eyes through which we read the book of nature?

The historical discussions in the previous chapters have indicated the wisdom of Albert Einstein's famous warning, "Religion without science is blind."[8] In the first few centuries of the Christian era the Church taught that the earth was flat, that the universe was modeled after the ark of the covenant—clearly a blind science. These follies demonstrate that it is simply not possible to build a credible scientific description of the universe using only the Bible. The Aristotelian influence, which was external to the Christian tradition, improved the scientific literacy of the Church immensely, but when that scientific theory became woven into the fabric of theology, it had to be extracted very carefully to avoid destroying the tapestry of religion.

The lesson of the Galileo affair is clear: It is not safe to use biblical proof texts as support for particular scientific ideas. We are not that much smarter than the Christian scholars from the time of Galileo—men like Luther, Calvin, Bellarmine, and so on. If Martin Luther could not find the correct scientific worldview in the Bible, then what makes us think we can? The truth is that we cannot, and we must be prepared to recognize science as the authority on such questions.

The scientific creationists present their case on two fronts:

1. When addressing the Church, they argue that it is essential that the Bible be interpreted literally, which will always demonstrate the exclusive truth of their particular explanation of origins. Such a perspective on the Bible is essential, they argue, to avoid the long slide into apostasy that has characterized all religious groups that disagree with them. As a leader of this movement writes,

> The sad fact is that evolutionism has also deeply affected evangelical schools and churches. After all, even

---

8. Albert Einstein, "Science and Religion," in *Out of My Later Years* (Secaucus, N.J.: Citadel Press, 1956), 26. In this essay Einstein is arguing that the "aspiration towards truth and understanding" that motivates the scientist "springs from the sphere of religion." Science is "lame" without that faith. In the same way he argues that religion needs to learn from science "what means will contribute to the attainment of the goals that it has set up." Without this knowledge, religion is "blind."

modern ultra-liberal theological schools (e.g., Harvard, Yale) and denominations (e.g., Methodist, Episcopalian) were once orthodox and zealous for the Scriptures. These institutions have traveled down the road of compromise with evolutionary humanism farther than most, but many evangelicals today seem to have embarked on the same icy road, unaware of the dangers ahead and impatient with those who would warn them.

Evangelicals . . . generally "dare not call it compromise" and perhaps are not even aware of it, but compromise they have, in many, many instances. Some have accepted full blown theistic evolution, but many more believe in either "progressive creation" or "reconstructive creation" (i.e., the so-called Gap Theory). . . .

That these systems (theistic evolution, etc.) are actually dangerous compromises rather than legitimate interpretations of Scripture should be obvious for anyone committed to the proposition that the Bible really is the inerrant Word of God.[9]

This eloquent passage, reminiscent of the warnings against the dangers of Copernicanism, is very persuasive. Certainly conservative Christian colleges do not want to embrace the liberal theology of Harvard University. But we must remember that Harvard's once-conservative theology was buried deep under its green quadrants before Darwinism ever set foot on the campus. It was not evolution that destroyed Harvard's Christian witness; it was the secularization of society that was proceeding at a very healthy pace without the help of Charles Darwin. It was political evolution, not biological, that was inducing these mutations.

The author of the above passage goes on to indict many of the mainstream evangelical institutions because of their compromises: Wheaton, Gordon, Calvin, and Westmont colleges—the academic cream of the Christian College Coalition; InterVarsity Christian Press; the American Scientific Affiliation—an evangelical scientific organization, generally very well respected; and so on.

---

9. Morris, *Long War Against God*, 101-2.

2. In addition to the essentially religious arguments stated above, the scientific creationists have a second argument supposedly based entirely on science. In this argument, the creationists attempt to use the actual data of science to support their conclusions. Cloaked in this garb, the creationists begin to resemble mainstream scientists, who generally afford science a great deal of authority. As we will see later, however, the creationists do not really accept the independent authority of science without confirming scriptural corroboration.[10]

The scientific creationists believe that it is possible to argue directly from known scientific facts and theories that their particular interpretation of origins is valid. In fact, the entire scientific creationist movement is motivated by the desire to create an apparently nonreligious, scientifically supported theory of origins that can successfully challenge the modern evolutionary theories without invoking the support of religion.

One of the most attractive features of this theory of origins is the remarkable correlation between the biblical account of creation and the scientific account, as the creationists present it. There are thus two separate pillars of support, each complementing the other and providing additional insight. That there should simultaneously be two separate authorities supporting the same worldview is the best possible situation; if you tend to favor scientific explanations, you can find comfort in the additional support from religion; if you prefer religious explanations, you can find comfort in the scientific vindication. In either case there will certainly be no conflict between the two.

The scientific creationist worldview thus provides the same kind of metaphysical underpinning that the medieval worldview provided for Christians in the late Middle Ages. Their worldview was constructed from a synthesis of Scripture and secular science, which were found to be complementary. Their

---

10. The literature of the creationists, particularly the material written for Christian audiences, makes it clear that they accept the Bible as the final authority on matters scientific. If science is in disagreement with the Bible, then that science is in error. The only authority that science might have would deal with scientific questions that had no connection with anything in the Bible. In fact, many of the creationists argue that Christians should be skeptical of modern science because many scientists are "unbelievers."

worldview was one of harmony; and there were no conflicts, at least until Galileo came along.

The medieval worldview is long gone. Biblical scholars now challenge the exegetical approach of their medieval predecessors as woefully inadequate. The Bible, they argue, does not teach that the earth is fixed in the center of the universe.

History will judge the worldview of the scientific creationists. Will the verdict be the same? Will biblical scholars look back at these decades and lament that a very particular approach to the Scriptures distorted its message? Will the scientific community look back and remark about the incredibly naive notions that almost made their way into science?

These are the two fundamental questions: (1) Does a proper interpretation of the Bible require the adoption of a particular scientific worldview? (2) Do the facts of science support the theory of origins known as scientific creationism?

The next two chapters will address each of these questions individually.

7

Scientific Creationism—
the Biblical Perspective

· · · · ·

*What is the ultimate solution to the origin of
the Universe? The answers provided by the
astronomers are disconcerting and remarkable. Most of all is the fact that in science, as
in the Bible, the world begins with an act of
creation.*

Robert Jastrow, Astronomer

· · · · ·

When Isaac Newton's theory of gravitation was fully worked
out, it seemed clear to everyone that the universe must be both
infinitely large and static. It must have no boundary, and it
must not be changing in any significant, large-scale way.

Both of these ideas were attractive from a number of perspectives. An *infinite* universe meant that astronomers didn't
have to worry about some unknown region beyond the edge of
the universe. It also meant that God the Creator must be infinite. A *static* universe meant that astronomers did not have to
figure out any complex theories of cosmic evolution; more important, it also meant that the universe today was basically the
same as the one God had created in 3998 B.C., which was Isaac
Newton's estimate of the date of the creation of the universe,
based on his analysis of the biblical genealogies.

Newton's theories seemed to be thoroughly confirmed by
observation; no change was observed in the heavens, and they
did appear to be without boundary. In fact, the very concept of

a boundary to the universe seemed self-evidently false. The infinite static universe became the ruling scientific paradigm—an assumed theoretical framework that is accepted without question and into which all new ideas must be integrated.

Einstein developed his general theory of relativity in 1915 within the paradigm of the static infinite universe. Thus, he was dismayed to find out that his theory suggested the universe was neither static nor infinite. His new theory was clear—the universe was either expanding or contracting. But all the astronomers with their huge telescopes assured him that the universe was static. The ruling paradigm was so strong that Einstein could not conceive of challenging it. So he added a fudge factor called the cosmological constant to his theory. It changed his general theory of relativity from beautiful to ugly, but it achieved the desired conformity to the static universe paradigm. Later he referred to this cosmological constant as the "greatest blunder of my career."

In 1929, Edwin Hubble, for whom the famous telescope was named, discovered that the universe was expanding. Einstein greeted the discovery with elation. He removed the cosmological constant from his theory and restored its original beauty.

Theory and experiment, the two legs of science, now stood firmly together in agreement: the universe was *changing*. But how was it changing? Much to the astonishment of the scientific community, it was getting *bigger*. The universe was *expanding*. And not only was it presently expanding—it had been expanding since the beginning of time. If you ran the cosmic clock in reverse, the universe shrank up into a tiny speck. This speck was the original universe all bundled up into a very compact package, smaller than a pea. This crazy idea—and it surely was crazy—was named the "big noise" by its developer, a Belgian priest/scientist named Georges Lemaître.

This crazy big noise idea was not embraced with open arms. Astrophysicist Fred Hoyle, who would later win the Nobel prize, insultingly referred to the new theory as the "big bang," an originally nasty name that stuck. The big bang was challenged and vigorously opposed for decades. Alternate theories were suggested in an attempt to get away from this *evolving* universe. But finally the observational and theoretical evidence mounted to the point where it was no longer possible to challenge the bizarre idea. All opposing theories yielded under the onslaught of important new observations, and the big bang emerged triumphant.

The scientific community was forced to admit that the universe was not eternal; they were driven to the inescapable conclusion that it had been created at some point in the past. The grandest collection of scientific minds in history had labored for a half century, only to confirm what Moses had written thousands of years earlier: "In the beginning God created the heavens and the earth."

Contemporary astronomer Robert Jastrow, himself an agnostic, puts it like this: "For the scientist who has lived by his faith in the power of reason, the story ends like a bad dream. He has scaled the mountains of ignorance; he is about to conquer the highest peak; as he pulls himself over the final rock, he is greeted by a band of theologians who have been sitting there for centuries."[1]

Outline

This is the first of three chapters that will examine the various dimensions of scientific creationism or, less commonly, creation science. In this chapter we will argue that scientific creationism is not derived from a literal reading of the Bible, but rather derives from the belief that evolution is a profound evil that must be attacked with all possible weapons. The Bible is accordingly transformed into such a weapon by a very narrow and unwarranted interpretation of certain passages that are made to appear contrary to evolutionary theory. The antievolutionary perspective of the Bible thus emerges from an *eisegesis* (reading into the Bible), rather than from an *exegesis* (finding the intended meaning of the Bible).

To demonstrate the eisegetical nature of the creationists' biblical foundations, we will consider some of the views that

---

1. Robert Jastrow, *God and the Astronomers* (New York: W. W. Norton and Co., 1978), 116.

other biblical literalists have on the meaning of the Genesis account. We will see that there are several different interpretations of the literal meaning of Genesis, thus refuting the creationists' claim that anyone who "takes God at His Word" by believing the literal truth of the Bible will share their antievolutionary views.

A Red Herring

Bloodhounds have been used throughout history to track escaping criminals, who knew they must confuse the bloodhounds if they were to be successful in their escape. One of the tricks the criminal employed was to drag a strong-smelling red herring across their trail, which would cause the bloodhound to lose the scent and become confused by this much stronger smell. Thus, red herring has come to mean anything brought into an argument to distract and confuse the discussion.

The issue of creation versus evolution is a modern example of a red herring. The very fact that the controversy is known so familiarly by this phrase "creation versus evolution" attests to this fact, since two *independent* concepts are set up in *opposition* to one another. The concept of creation is fundamentally theological; it addresses the relationship between the created world and the Creator. Throughout the history of philosophy and theology, the doctrine of creation has been a profound metaphysical statement about the ultimate nature of the universe: Is it eternal or was it created? Does it need God to sustain it? How is the creation related to God? What aspects of God can be discerned in the details of the creation? And so on.

Creation should not be understood as a detailed theory about the exact processes God used to bring the world into existence. In the same way, the various theories of evolution have never stated that God does not exist, or that He is powerless or irrelevant. In most cases, evolution per se says *nothing* that is of theological relevance. This can be demonstrated very easily by simply consulting the relevant scientific journals that report on developments and discoveries relevant to evolutionary theory. In *no* articles in *any* of these journals will one find any discussion of theological topics. The journals will report on new fossil findings, experiments to try and understand the development of RNA or DNA, the discovery of new species, new findings in genetics, and so on. Nowhere will there be an article in a legitimate scientific journal discussing whether or not all of these scientific ideas confirm or dispute the notion of God as the Creator of the universe and of life. That topic is simply outside the scope of science. When individual scientists choose to make comments about the theological implications of their work—and there are some scientists who like to do this—they are moving beyond their expertise and training into the field of theology and should be evaluated according to criteria appropriate to theology, rather than science.

Evolution is not a religious doctrine, nor is it an antireligious doctrine. It is a collection of theories that purport to show how certain very complex things in our universe, from stars to hummingbirds to people, have evolved from much simpler things.

So how is it that two independent concepts—creation and evolution—find themselves pitted against one another as if they are incompatible and one must choose between them?

The truth of the matter is that creation should be understood as a theological doctrine and evolution as a scientific one. An affirmation of creation should not entail the adoption of a particular set of scientific theories. Similarly, an affirmation of evolution should not entail any particular theological stance. They are unrelated concepts that cannot be incompatible, because they are not related to one another.

Nevertheless, in the popular media this argument has become familiar as the creation versus evolution controversy, so we will, for clarity, discuss it in those terms. The reader must keep in mind, however, that *creation* will frequently be used in the narrow sense of a particular scientific theory of origins that is, for all practical purposes, devoid of any significant theological dimension.

We will argue later that many different scientific explanations of origins are completely compatible with a genuine creationist position.

Scientific Creationism Versus the Genesis Account

The scientific creationists sing only one part in the great evangelical choir, but they sing so loudly and so frequently that they are often mistaken for the whole chorus. In fact, there are many biblical literalists who are, by definition, both fundamentalist and creationist but whose views on origins differ significantly from those of the scientific creationists. As stated earlier, not everyone who chooses to interpret the Bible from a position of literalism will agree on what the Bible is trying to say.

The scientific creationists, however, have a unique approach to this complex problem. They argue that the true facts of science demonstrate the truth of the biblical record. Writing as scientific, rather than religious, authorities, they are attempting to appeal to the modern worldview. Furthermore, they argue that belief in the Genesis account of creation is no longer a matter of faith, for all the scientific evidence clearly demonstrates its truth. Thus, they argue, competent scientists will subscribe to their particular theory of origins whether or not they believe in the Bible, simply on the basis of the evidence. If particularly cantankerous scientists fail to see the creationists' point, that simply means that they must be a part of Satan's grand deception.

With a professional scientific organization, an institute for creation "research," a "scientific" journal, and a publishing house behind them, the scientific creationists represent a formidable voice of authority. Furthermore, the leading creationists are prolific authors and have produced a vast literature that seems to totally dominate the field of science and religion. Christian bookstores frequently contain only one perspective on modern science and the Genesis account, not because that is all that exists, but because that perspective markets itself so aggressively.

With this in mind, the discussion in this chapter will be limited to just that version of creationism that calls itself *scientific* creationism. This particular viewpoint is remarkable on two accounts: (1) it contains a broad-based attack on almost *all* of modern science, not just the "man from apes" issue that historically has been the focus of disagreement; and (2) its advocates include some scientists, which gives it an extra margin of credibility in our modern scientific world.

(For the sake of simplicity and literary stewardship, the word *creationist* will be used to represent *scientific creationist* in the rest of this chapter.)

The creationists' theory of origins makes an honest attempt to be a complete scientific theory, in that it attempts to deal with all the relevant data. Such a complete theory *must* accommodate all of the relevant data, whether it fits comfortably into the theory or not. It is not acceptable for a scientific theory to propose, for example, that the earth is only 10,000 years old, unless that theory is also capable of explaining those measurements of the age of the earth that yield values in the millions or even billions of years. It is not acceptable to propose that all the stars were created at the same time without explaining why new stars seem to appear from time to time. It is not acceptable to maintain that humans are unrelated in any way to other animals without explaining why there appear to be so many similarities.

The creationists thus demonstrate a certain integrity in their approach by their willingness to at least acknowledge the diversity of phenomena that are difficult to reconcile with their theories. They are not like the timid critics of Galileo who refused even to look through his telescope; creationists boldly hold the telescope up to their eyes, confident that they can fit any anticipated observations into their theory of origins. Nor are they like the critics of geology who once argued that God put the fossils in the ground to test the faith of the Christian.

The attempt by the creationists to provide a complete theory has led to an extraordinarily broad attack on almost all of modern science. When the subtle and far-reaching implications of their theories are fully worked out, many problems emerge that require a radical reinterpretation of a variety of natural phenomena. This is not in any sense a criticism of their theories; in fact, all great scientific revolutions have shared this important feature. It does, however, suggest that caution be exercised in embracing a particular idea, such as the recent creation of the earth. If this idea is adopted, with all its associated theoretical baggage, many ideas fundamental to physics, chemistry, geology, astronomy, biology, and so on must be discarded.

This chapter will examine the biblical foundations of the modern creationist movement. The creationists have developed a very specific theory of origins they claim is based on the Genesis account of creation. But we will see that their approach to the Scriptures is not entirely objective. In fact, their exegesis of Genesis seems to be motivated by a search for antievolutionary scriptural ammunition, rather than by an objective attempt to determine precisely what the writer of Genesis was trying to communicate. Even though they do not appear to recognize it, their one-dimensional, antievolutionary worldview has led them to untenable positions in science, theology, and biblical interpretation.

Briefly, then, here are the tenets of creationism. They are taken from Arkansas's Act 590, which was an attempt to introduce creationism into the Arkansas high school curriculum.

Creation-science means the scientific evidences and related inferences that indicate:

1. sudden creation of the universe, energy, and life from nothing
2. the insufficiency of mutation and natural selection in bringing about development of all living kinds from a single organism
3. changes only within fixed limits of originally created kinds of plants and animals
4. separate ancestry for man and apes
5. explanation of the earth's geology by catastrophism, including the occurrence of a worldwide flood
6. a relatively recent inception of the earth and living kinds

These six tenets represent an attempted scientific summary of the first few chapters of Genesis and the implications that emerge indirectly from that source. They represent the essential content of all versions of creationism. If attempts to move creationism into the classroom are successful, the above concepts will be taught alongside the theory of evolution as a scientifically viable alternative.

We will now look at these tenets individually from a biblical point of view and see whether or not they represent the only possible, or even most reasonable, interpretation of the Genesis creation account. We will see that the interpretation placed on some of the verses in Genesis is not strictly justified and indicates, rather, that the creationists are attempting to magnify the apparent conflict between the Bible and the general consensus of modern science.

1. Sudden creation of the universe, and life, from nothing. The Genesis account says, "In the beginning God created the heavens and the earth" (Gen. 1:1). The implication is that the universe, although that was not a concept familiar to the Hebrews, was created from nothing. But this is not the case for "life." The Genesis account states, "Then God said, 'Let the land *produce* vegetation' . . . 'Let the land *produce* living creatures'" (1:11, 24, emphasis added). Animal and plant life are thus not created from nothing; rather they *emerge from the land by an unspecified process.* Thus the creationists are insisting on a particular interpretation of these difficult passages, one that ensures a conflict with evolutionary theories about the origin of plants and animals.

For example, if one is willing to let the "days" be long periods of time, the "production of living creatures" could indeed be the evolutionary processes that modern biology believes are responsible. The ancient Hebrews, in fact, believed that living creatures could emerge spontaneously[2] from nonliving material, a belief that wasn't disproved until the 19th century, when Pasteur showed that spontaneous generation does not occur.

If we assume the writer of Genesis is communicating within the context of the Hebrew worldview, then the creation ac-

---

2. Westermann says, for example, "The meaning of 'the bringing forth' is primarily: 'Let something which is within come out' . . . The background is the widespread image of Mother Earth, the earth as the bearer of all life and all the vegetation." From Claus Westermann, *Genesis 1-11: A Commentary* (Minneapolis: Augsburg Publishing House, 1974), 125. It must be pointed out that the ancient Hebrews were not interested in purely scientific explanations, so we cannot equate their belief about "Mother Earth" with the 18th-century concept of spontaneous generation. Nevertheless, they did have explanations for natural phenomena, and it would seem their concept of the origin of some life forms involved the earth's simply bringing forth life. The generative abilities of the earth were, of course, derived from the "Word" of Yahweh.

count is describing the emergence of animal and plant life from nonliving material through the generative potential placed in the earth by the Creator.[3] This is an idea that is not only compatible with modern evolutionary theories but actually in harmony with them.

2. The insufficiency of mutation and natural selection in bringing about development of all living kinds from a single organism. This idea is not even loosely based on the Genesis account. Mutation and natural selection are modern concepts that would have been totally foreign to the writer of Genesis. Furthermore, this argument at present is unadulterated God of the gaps. The whole topic is a big, tangled mystery that many evolutionary biologists are trying to unravel. On the level of microevolution, the interaction of mutation and natural selection is well understood; but on the larger scale, the clarity vanishes into a fog that has not yet begun to lift.

3. Changes only within fixed limits of originally created kinds of plants and animals. The creationists place a large emphasis on the word *kind* (Hebrew *min*). They argue that *min* represents some kind of divinely ordained limit on the potential variation available to an original species.[4] For example, they suggest that *dog* may be one of the original *kinds*. The fixed limits imposed by *min* on the dog kind prevent it from ever evolving into nondog. It is possible for a single created pair of original dogs to evolve into collies, dachshunds, retrievers, Dobermans, perhaps into wolves and foxes, but not into cats or horses.

The creationists have been unable to determine the limits imposed by *min*, but they insist on it, nevertheless, because it refutes evolution. If *min* is a viable biological concept, then it ought to correlate with some known principles of biology. But if we look closely at the creation account, we can see that this is not what it is saying at all. In Gen. 1:11 we read, "Then God

---

3. We must point out that the Hebrews would never have phrased these explanations in this way, because they did not use scientific explanations. (See the preceding reference.) Nevertheless, the creationists do assume that Genesis is a scientific account, so we must attempt to formulate these ideas in modern scientific parlance to see how they resonate with our modern theories.

4. Henry Morris, *The Genesis Record* (San Diego: Creation-Life Publishers, 1976), 63.

said, 'Let the land produce vegetation: seed-bearing plants and trees on the land that bear fruit with seed in it, according to their various kinds.'" The implication here is that apple trees have apples growing on them; these apples contain seeds that can be used to produce more apple trees. Apples do not have orange seeds inside them. But this is not even in mild disagreement with an evolutionary origin for apple trees. Evolution does not claim that apples sometimes have orange seeds in them. Evolution understands that all species have offspring that differ only *slightly,* if at all, from their parents, a notion that would certainly give the writer of Genesis no problem.

Even if apple trees did evolve slowly from orange trees, each individual fruit from all of the countless intermediate transitional trees contained seeds that would have produced after its kind. Because of the incredibly slow pace of evolutionary development, all offspring, whether apples or puppies, look like their parents. There is no uncrossable evolutionary barrier suggested by the biblical *kind.* All that can be legitimately inferred from this verse is that offspring look like their parents; apples contain apple seeds, and everyone agrees on that.

The creationists have assigned a very elaborate biological thesis to this verse, one that is clearly not based on a careful exegesis, but rather on their need to refute all forms of evolution with biblical proof texts.

4. Separate ancestry for man and apes. This is the most controversial element in the entire theory of evolution. Did we evolve from ape-like ancestors? Or were we created in more or less the same form we possess today? All interpretations of the Genesis account recognize that one of its primary messages is that humans are in a distinctly different class from animals. We are not just the smartest of the animals or the monkeys with the biggest brains. The difference, according to the Genesis account, is that we exist in the image of God. We are unique in that we alone have this special relationship with our Creator.

But is this uniqueness physical or spiritual? If it is spiritual, and most theologians would argue that it is, then there is absolutely no problem associated with the origin of our physical bodies. In fact, it is universally acknowledged that our physical bodies are not really much different from many of the other animals. Zoology students in universities everywhere memorize the skeleton of the cat because it is so similar to that of the human. And primates are even more similar (but their skeletons are too big and too expensive for the biology lab).

However it was that humans came to be "in the image of God," it most certainly had nothing to do with the development of our physical bodies. Some biblical scholars have attempted to harmonize the evolutionary origin of man with the biblical account by assuming that the image of God emerged in the developing human species at some appropriate point, perhaps in association with the development of intelligence. While this may not be the most straightforward interpretation of the Genesis account, it does achieve some degree of reconciliation without destroying the essential truth of the text. At the very least, it represents an alternative to the strict creationist interpretation and demonstrates that conflict is not essential.

5. Explanation of the earth's geology by catastrophism, including the occurrence of a worldwide flood. The modern creationist movement started with the publication of *The Genesis Flood* in 1961. This influential book argues that the biblical flood was not a local flood and that the entire geological column and the fossils it contains, were laid down by sedimentary processes associated with the Flood. The Flood has become the scientific fairy godmother of creationism. No matter how complicated the problem, an appeal to the Flood can untangle the difficulty. "There is no observational fact imaginable which cannot, one way or another, be made to fit the creation model."[5]

This represents an astonishing faith on the part of the creationists. It is impossible, they boast, to even *imagine* something that would change their minds. What if all the missing links were discovered? What if a drawing of the constellations that could only have happened a million years ago turned up on the wall of some cave? What if the synthesis of life became so well understood that it was included as an experiment in chemistry

---

5. Henry Morris, *Scientific Creationism* (San Diego: Creation-Life Publishers, 1974), 10.

sets? Is there *no* scientific discovery that might dislodge some of their confidence?

Flood geology is not a part of the creation account. It is added to account for the apparent evolutionary sequence that even the creationists acknowledge is easily visible in the geological record. That is, it attempts to explain why simple animals are found in lower parts of the geological column and complex ones at the top. The creationist explanation is that the simple animals, being simple of mind as well as structure, didn't know enough to run to higher elevations to escape being buried by the rising flood waters. Thus they got buried at the bottom of the hill, while the smarter animals ran to the top before they got buried.

The implausibility of this argument points up the weakness in the creationist case. In fact, the extraordinary scientific problems associated with the Flood story in Genesis, not the least of which is the total absence of geological evidence for a *worldwide* flood, have led many biblical scholars, and practically all scientists, to conclude that the Flood must have been a local one.

This is a fascinating topic, but one that cannot detain us here. Suffice it to say that the creationist theory of origins requires an extraordinary supplement in the form of a far-reaching flood theory that, like their exegesis of Genesis 1 and 2, goes far beyond anything that can reasonably be inferred from the scriptural accounts. The interested reader is encouraged to consult *The Christian View of Science and Scripture* by influential evangelical scholar Bernard Ramm for a complete discussion.

6. A relatively recent inception of the earth and living kinds. The doctrine of a recent creation is essential to the creationists because evolutionary processes, whether they be biological, geological, or physical, require vast eons of time in which to accomplish their slow task. But biblical scholars do not agree on the precise timing of creation. As we mentioned earlier, there are many alternate interpretations of Genesis that allow the universe to be old.

Whatever one's approach to Scripture, it cannot be denied that the meaning of "day" is open to some interpretation. It is also possible that there may be gaps of uncertain duration in the creation account. In any event it is clear that the Bible does not state categorically that the earth is young. The gap theory is certainly a reasonable interpretation but not the only one.

The popular day-age theory is one way out of the apparent dilemma faced by the concordists at this point. The Hebrew word for day is *yom*. *Yom* usually means an ordinary day, such as we have on our calendar. But it can also mean "a long time," which is how it is used in Josh. 24:7, in which Joshua tells the Israelites that they "lived in the desert for a long time *[yom]*." In Gen. 4:3 we read, "In the course of time *[yom]* Cain brought some of the fruits of the soil as an offering to the Lord." Isa. 4:2 reads, "In that day *[yom]* the Branch of the Lord will be beautiful and glorious."

H. Orton Wiley says the following:

> The Hebrew word *yom* which is translated "day" occurs no less than 1,480 times in the Old Testament, and is translated by something over fifty different words, including such terms as *time, life, today, age, forever, continually* and *perpetually*. With such a flexible use of the original term, it is impossible to either dogmatize or to demand unswerving restriction to one of those meanings.[6]

It is clear that *yom* can have a variety of meanings, only one of which is a 24-hour day. The context of Genesis indicates that this may be the meaning intended in the creation story, but it is not *clear* that this is the case. It is certainly not demanded. Furthermore, the gap theory, presented in the popular Scofield reference Bible, of which more than 20 million copies were sold, is another way to avoid the young earth problem. Even among fundamentalist biblical scholars who are all, of course, biblical literalists, there is considerable disagreement on this point.

Charles Ryrie, former professor at Dallas Theological Seminary, concedes that it is possible to read an old earth into the creation account: "Thus the original unfashioned earth might have been old."[7] Norman Geisler, ardent fundamentalist apolo-

---

6. H. Orton Wiley, *Christian Theology* (Kansas City: Beacon Hill Press, 1940), 1:455.

gist and witness for the creationists at the Arkansas trial, addresses this issue directly in his manifesto *When Skeptics Ask:*

> Of course, there are many Creationists who argue for an old earth. Biblically, this position, that the word for *day* is used for more than 24 hours even in Genesis 2:4, the events of the sixth day surely took more than 24 hours, and Hebrews 4:4-5 implies that God is still in His seventh day rest. If the seventh day can be long, then the others could too. Scientifically, this view does not require any novel theories to explain the evidence . . . The old earth view seems to fit the evidence better and *causes no problem with the Bible.*[8]

Norman Geisler is a dean of the Liberty Center for Research and Scholarship at Liberty University in Lynchburg, Va., headed by one of the most articulate advocates of modern fundamentalism, Jerry Falwell. Geisler is a former professor at Dallas Theological Seminary, the academic heart of fundamentalism. He has an impeccable fundamentalist pedigree, yet he disagrees with the creationists on the age of the earth as determined from the Bible.

In fact, even William Jennings Bryan did not necessarily believe the Bible taught that the earth was young. When the besieged Bryan admitted this under Darrow's merciless cross-examination, the creationists could be heard to gasp, and Bryan's star began to fall in the great sky of fundamentalism.

The truth is that it is simply not possible to determine the age of the universe from the Bible. "In the beginning God created" is clear and true, but when this took place simply cannot be determined from the Bible. It is one of those questions science has to answer, if it can be answered at all. And, as we will see in the next chapter, the weakest link in the entire creationist program is the age of the universe. But it is their best argument against evolution.

---

7. Charles Ryrie, *Basic Theology* (Wheaton, Ill.: Victor Books, 1988), 188.
8. Norman Geisler, *When Skeptics Ask* (Wheaton, Ill.: Victor Books, 1990), 230, emphasis added.

Conclusion

We can see from this analysis that the creationists have developed an interpretation of the creation account designed to maximize conflict with any and all evolutionary theories. It is clear that their exegesis, which is really an eisegesis, is guided by the conviction that the biblical record must contain a thorough refutation of evolution. The exegesis is not guided by an attempt to understand what the biblical writer was trying to communicate, nor by what the biblical account should mean to the modern reader. Certainly the writer of Genesis was not trying to provide scriptural ammunition for a war that was thousands of years in the future.

The preceding should demonstrate that reading the Bible through the eyes of fundamentalism does not necessitate finding scientific creationism within its pages. It is certainly reasonable to suspend judgment on an issue like the age of the earth or the origin of animal life until such time as those questions are fully answered. We can look back at the Galileo incident and easily see that the Church would have been the wiser if it had carefully determined which matters were relevant to faith in the gospel of Jesus Christ and which were not. Certainly the immovability of the earth seems like an unimportant doctrine today; if only it had been recognized as unimportant 300 years ago.

We must now recognize that many of the issues the creationists are using as tests of orthodoxy are similarly irrelevant. If the earth is only 10,000 years old, then science will eventually come to that conclusion. On the other hand, if the earth is billions of years old, as so many independent measurements demonstrate, why insist that the Bible teaches otherwise?

How Should We Then Read?

There are two conclusions to be drawn from the preceding discussion: (1) The creationists are reading their own particular antievolutionary worldview into the Bible. A straightforward exegesis of the creation account does not justify their dogmatic stance on origins. (2) It is possible to reconcile a literal interpretation of the Genesis account with much of evolutionary theory.

Biblical literalism is thus not entirely antievolutionary, just as we now recognize that it is not anti-Copernican *even though that wasn't clear four centuries ago.*

There is a serious question, however, as to whether it is even appropriate to treat the creation story in Genesis as a scientific account. The creationists have assumed the first chapter of Genesis is scientific literature. They have assumed the writer meant to communicate scientific truth. They have assumed he wrote from the perspective of our modern Western worldview rather than from the perspective of his own Hebrew worldview. They have assumed that what he wrote was not conditioned in any way by the prevailing primitive worldview of the ancient Hebrews. And they have assumed the account must, of necessity, disagree with evolutionary theory on every point. What is the basis for these assumptions?

In the next chapter we will consider the nature of the Genesis account in an effort to determine how its author intended it to be interpreted.

8

How Should We Then Read?

• • • • •

There is not and never can be any opposition between science and religion, any more than there can be between grammar and religion.

H. Orton Wiley

• • • • •

In the beginning they sought freedom—freedom of thought, freedom of expression, freedom of worship.

So they came to the New World,

And it was a great day.

And they said, "Let us build a new country, where we can be free from political masters and worship as our conscience leads."

So they built a new country,

And it was a second great day.

Then they said, "Let us join together for security and become united as one nation under God."

So they joined political hands,

And it was a third great day.

Then they said, "Let us ensure that freedom will always rule, in this our new land, our home where freedom reigns."

So they forged documents to guarantee the basic rights of citizens, to ensure each man's freedom to worship his God.

And it was a fourth great day.

Then they said, "Let us write a constitution that will keep our rulers honest."

So their greatest thinkers gathered to set down in writing how a free people should be governed,

155

And it was a fifth great day.

And the country grew and prospered until someone asked,
"But why are black people not free like whites? Where is
their freedom in this land of the free?"

So they struggled mightily to free the black people,

And it was a sixth great day.

And on the seventh day the great country stopped and rested
and praised their God for His mercy and care.

Outline

This chapter will argue that the Bible cannot be properly
understood without consideration of the perspectives and
worldviews of its authors. In particular, we will argue that the
Genesis account of creation contains many elements of the
primitive Hebrew cosmology that have been replaced by later
developments in science.

But these scientific inaccuracies pose a problem for those
who subscribe to the doctrine of plenary verbal inspiration of
the Scriptures, which requires that every statement in the Bible
must be entirely factual since it was essentially written by God.
We will argue that this is an untenable doctrine of inspiration
that must be replaced by one in which it is the *writers* who are
inspired to communicate profound theological truth within the
context, and limitations, of their own worldview.

Within the framework of this dynamical theory of inspiration the Genesis account comes alive, not as a source for science
that was millennia ahead of its time, but as a profound expression of the Hebrew faith in God as the Creator and Sustainer of
the world.

The Bible as Literature

The reader will recognize the passage that opened this
chapter as a poetic account of the development of the United
States. Because we know the history of the United States, we
easily recognize that the account does not describe seven consecutive ordinary days during which the country was taken
from the unclaimed New World through the Civil Rights movement. But, if convinced to read the account literally, we would

have to assume that this poetic account describes a week of intense political activity sometime around the founding of the United States. But why would anyone insist that such a document be taken literally in order for it to be true? It seems clear that it is poetic and that its truth is not *newspaper* truth but *profound* truth.

In much the same way, the scientist who is a Christian knows the Genesis account does not contain newspaper truth. The scientist's knowledge of the world makes it clear that the Genesis story is not a transcription of material reviewed on a videotape by an objective reporter. The Genesis account is a moving and deeply spiritual testimony of the profound truths contained in the statement, "In the beginning God." The writer is not a dispassionate scientific scribe with no interest in the subject, but rather a deeply involved and inspired author who is communicating profound truths that are deeply meaningful to him. The events described cannot be eyewitness accounts, because the details do not fit what we know about the world being described.

But the creation story is not an account of details; details are for the newspaper. This is an account of God the Creator making the world. Do we really think we can describe that process with our limited intellectual and linguistic capacities? The true nature of God's creative activity cannot be understood by beings as culturally and linguistically limited as we are. Even if eyewitnesses were present to describe "the creation of the heaven and earth," they would be unable to communicate that spectacle, because there would be no words with meanings appropriate to the occasion.

The interpretation of great literature requires great effort, as we have all painfully experienced while studying Shakespeare in our high school English classes. To lift a document out of a different culture, different language, and different worldview and try to figure out what it is saying is a complex task. The words do not translate directly, so shades of meaning are always lost. The assumed cultural literacy of the intended reader is no longer a given. The categories and assumptions of the worldview make theoretical concepts almost incomprehensible.

And yet there is much value in the study of such literature, particularly in the case of the Bible.

Fortunately, the Bible is such an important book that many scholars have devoted their lives to its study, spending years learning the original languages, cultures, and worldviews in which it was written. And these scholars have, for the most part, reached a consensus on the interpretation of the first chapter of Genesis.

In this chapter we will look very briefly at the Genesis account of creation from two perspectives: (1) We will consider the account as if it contained newspaper truth and show that this approach is simply not credible; (2) then we will examine the internal structure and context of the account to see whether we can gain any insight into what the writer was trying to communicate.

The Creation Account as Newspaper Truth

One way to approach the Genesis account is the same way that we would approach a modern newspaper published in our hometown. Such a newspaper might contain a report of a very controversial decision reached by the authorities to allow a religious group to meet in a local high school provided that they made an effort to "make persons of all faiths welcome in their meeting." As a resident of this town, you might be quite interested in the story, and it would be easy for you to understand the story for a number of reasons: (1) it is written in your language, (2) the person writing it has essentially the same cultural background as you, (3) you are familiar with the issue from prior stories in previous newspapers and (4) you know many of the background details already, so they do not need to be explained again.

Now suppose that you took this same account to a different culture, say a Buddhist community in Asia, and watched them attempt to translate it and then decipher it. All of a sudden the simple story has become unimaginably complex. Loaded words like *faiths* and *denominations* are suddenly very complex and perhaps even meaningless in this different culture, which might not even have corresponding words to describe these concepts.

In a different country where democratic politics was not practiced, the problem would seem trivial. In a country where education was controlled by the church, the issue would seem irrelevant. The apparently straightforward account would not make sense if interpreted within the context of a radically different worldview. By the same token, if you were to pick up a Japanese newspaper and read an account of an employee of the Sony Corporation who brought shame on his family by quitting the company and going to work for Toyota, you might be very confused about the relevant background issues that made this such a big deal.

In an analogous way, much of the Genesis account is difficult to interpret within the context of our modern worldview. Let us assume, for the sake of argument, that the writer of the Genesis account shares our modern worldview. This means he is aware of the contemporary description of the universe. He knows the earth is round and orbits the sun. He knows where and what stars are, how they shine, and that our sun is an ordinary star. He knows the moon is just a big rock. He knows the earth is billions of years old. He knows many things about the detailed structure of the modern universe.

If we assume that our hypothetical writer—Moses the American—is writing within the context of our modern worldview, then we will find his account of the creation of the world to be full of misunderstandings, scientific inaccuracies, and some things that border on nonsense.

Reading the Genesis account as a straightforward historical narrative presumed to accurately and scientifically describe God's creative activity over the course of six consecutive days will present the reader with a number of problems:

1. In Gen. 1:4 we read that "God . . . separated the light from the darkness." Based on the modern understanding of light, there is no meaning to an "unseparated" light/darkness mixture. To the Hebrews this meant, no doubt, that the regular cycle of day and night was now initiated. But the creation account, in harmony with local mythologies, seems to presume the existence of some uncreated primordial darkness that lay upon the "surface of the deep." The light, created later, was sep-

arated from this primordial darkness. This process of "separation" is not a scientifically meaningful event. In fact, the apparently symmetrical status of light and darkness is difficult to understand scientifically. Darkness is not a thing or a collection of things. It is the absence of the photons that are present in the light. We cannot make darkness; we can make only light.

2. In verses 6 through 8 we read of the creation of an "expanse" or firmament, which God calls "sky." This expanse separates the waters in the earthly bodies of water from those above the earth. Those above the earth are the sources of rain, snow, etc. The idea being expressed is that of something being placed in between the two waters, a restraining barrier to hold back the waters above. This cannot be the sky, however, as we understand it today, for the sky is not *under* the clouds. Most of what we call the sky, which is really just the atmosphere, is *above* the clouds, not below. The sky cannot separate the waters because it is not in between the waters.

3. In verse 14 we read that God put "lights in the expanse of the sky." These are, of course, the sun, moon, and stars. But none of these lights are in the sky. With the exception of the moon, they are all millions (or trillions) of miles away from our sky. Even the moon is far beyond the limit of the sky.

4. In verse 16 we read that "God made two great lights— the greater light to govern the day and the lesser light to govern the night." The "lesser light" is obviously the moon. But the moon is not a light at all; the moon is really just a big rock that reflects light from the sun. In fact, Saturn is a greater light than the moon; it just looks dimmer because it is further away. And, if we want to be completely accurate, we must recognize that the moon is out during the day several times each month.

5. The question also arises now as to how the first three days were defined, with no sun to mark their passage. In verse 5 we read, "And there was evening, and there was morning— the first day." How could there have been evening with no sunset, or morning with no sunrise?

6. And how could we have the earth with no sun? The earth as we know it revolves around the sun. How could it be stable without its sun? This would not have been a problem for

The earth goes around the sun. For them, the earth was stationary and the sun was just a great light placed in the sky.

the Hebrews, because they had no way of knowing the earth goes around the sun. For them, the earth was stationary and the sun was just a great light placed in the sky.

These problems, and many others, demonstrate the difficulty of extracting the Genesis account from the Hebrew worldview in which it was written and inserting it into our modern scientific worldview. The Hebrews had a very different concept of the universe than we have; these verses are describing God's creative work using concepts and categories specific to that universe.

As an example, we know from numerous studies of the worldview of the ancient Hebrews that they believed in a three-storied universe. They believed the earth was flat and that there was a huge, inverted bowl or dome sitting on this flat earth. (This was a very common primitive cosmology, one that is based on the most straightforward of observations. A modern observer, standing in the middle of a field at night under the stars, will observe the flat earth and the dome of heaven.) The lights in the heavens were all attached to this dome. There were windows in this dome, which could be opened to allow rain to come through. Thus we read in Gen. 7:11 of the "floodgates of the heavens" being opened to precipitate the flood of Noah.

The sky or expanse referred to in the creation account is this dome. The Hebrew word translated as "expanse" in Gen. 1:6 is *raqia*. It literally means "pounded-out thinness" or "spread-out thinness." Other uses of the word suggest that *raqia* is something that can be formed into a bowl by pounding. The notion of a solid sky was accepted by many cultures, including Western culture up to the scientific revolution. The only difference was that the solid sky of Aristotle was made of crystalline ether, rather than *raqia*.

The Hebrew worldview was that of a three-storied universe with a domed sky[1] filled with lights. There can be no doubt about this. The question then is the following: Is the cre-

---

1. Some recent translations acknowledge this cosmology in their choice of the English words used here to represent the "firmament." Westermann, for example, translates verse 6: "Let there be a solid vault in the middle of the waters so as to form a division between water and water." (See reference 2 in the preceding chapter.) The *New Revised Standard Version* uses the word "dome."

ation account written in the context of this primitive world-view? If it is, then does that make the Genesis creation account any less valuable?—any less *true?*

The Nature of Inspiration

To answer these questions requires that we consider the nature of biblical inspiration, a topic of considerable concern among Evangelicals. All Christians agree that the Bible is inspired, but inspiration means different things to different people. Most religious traditions have developed a doctrine of inspiration that conditions their approach to the Scriptures and thus determines to a large extent what they anticipate finding in those Scriptures. A legitimate doctrine of inspiration cannot be formulated, of course, simply by referring to those statements that Scripture makes about itself. This is circular reasoning. A doctrine of inspiration must be developed somewhat a priori in order to interpret what one reads. Typical views on inspiration include the following:

1. The doctrine of plenary verbal inspiration suggests that the biblical writers recorded the exact words of God when they wrote the Bible. The Bible is thus the product of a team of secretaries whose job it was to accurately record the statements of their boss. Supporters of this view argue that this is the only way to ensure that the Bible would be completely free from any kind of error. "It is by plenary (i.e., full) inspiration and by verbal (i.e., word-by-word) inspiration that God can objectively and accurately convey his Word to man."[2]

This view suggests that the human authors have an irrelevant role in the writing of Scripture. The Bible would be absolutely unchanged if God had written it himself, rather than having human authors transcribe it for Him. Inspiration is thus a divine phenomenon.

2. At the other end of the spectrum is the naturalistic theory, in which God plays no meaningful role at all. "The naturalistic theory holds that the Bible is inspired only in the sense that great writers and artists are inspired when they produce great

---

2. Morris, *Many Infallible Proofs*, 164.

works of literature or music or art. This theory in effect denies inspiration in any special biblical sense altogether."[3]

This view suggests that inspiration is really nothing more than motivation. To say the biblical authors were inspired to write is simply to say that they were motivated to write. And, of course, we know they were motivated or they would not have written!

Inspiration is thus a human phenomenon.

3. In between these two extremes lies the dynamical theory of inspiration. This theory suggests that God inspired the biblical writers by communicating some transcendent profound truth to them, which they then expressed within the context of their personal worldview. The profound and inspired truth is thus embedded in the author's words, but it is not equivalent to the author's words. "It is not the words of the Bible that are inspired but the writers of the scriptural books. God's action is personal, not mechanical; he seeks illumination to the minds of his servants, so that they think out the truth for themselves and make it their own."[4]

This view of inspiration suggests that the truth of the biblical message cannot always be found lying in plain view on top of the English text. For complicated passages it may be necessary to dig deeply to mine the inspired ore. It is a testimony to the strength of the biblical message that the gospel of salvation does lie in plain view for any honest reader to discover. But difficult passages require more effort. In particular, such passages will require that we uncover the worldview of the author and then determine what he meant when he wrote these passages. Theologian H. Ray Dunning puts it like this:

> In transforming the locus of inspiration from the writings to the writers, the dynamical theory implies the historical character of biblical language. In this it is significantly different from dictation or mechanical modes of inspiration. In the latter, the words are given directly to the writers so that the words are God's and not man's. . . .

---

3. Ibid., 163.
4. Alan Richardson, *The Bible in the Age of Science* (Philadelphia: Westminster Press, 1961), 68, in *Grace, Faith, and Holiness*, H. Ray Dunning (Kansas City: Beacon Hill Press of Kansas City, 1988), 69-70.

the crucial difference is that the words are the words of men who have their own understanding of what the words they use mean. That is, they are historically conditioned by the writer's intellectual, cultural, and societal milieu. They are even limited by his *factual* knowledge or lack of it. But none of this is essential to the authenticity of the thoughts. The issue becomes one of determining by careful exegetical methods the intention of the writer through analysis of his historical and linguistic context. The scrupulous attention biblical scholars give to the study of words is precisely to discover the original intention or understanding of the writer so as to accurately recover the truth that he was intending to convey and so determine what the text meant.[5]

The dynamical theory of inspiration is the most complicated. But we must take things as they are and not force them into simple categories for our own convenience. The Scriptures have a message to communicate; we must be wary of twisting that message to fit our own psychological preconceptions of what we would like that message to be.

The dynamical theory of inspiration undermines the entire biblical foundation of the scientific creationists. To see how it accomplishes this feat, let us consider an example of how a dynamically inspired account might be written.

The Nature of Dynamical Inspiration

As we stated earlier, one of the profound truths of the Genesis account is that it states that God is the Creator of all that is. Now this is a theological truth, one that transcends any particular worldview. As a totally generic statement of origins it would read, "Whatever you may think the world is, it was made by God." The significance of this is that (1) the world is not eternally self-existing, (2) the world did not arise from a purposeless nothing, and (3) the world does not find its origin in some polytheistic domestic warfare, as the Babylonians suggested. It has a monotheistic origin.

---

5. Dunning, *Grace, Faith, and Holiness*, 70-71.

This particular theological truth does not say anything about the details of the world; it simply says that it was made by God. Now suppose that a particular author was inspired to write that the universe was created by God. The dynamical theory of inspiration would suggest that this writer would communicate this profound, theological truth within the context of his own personal worldview. Thus, an ancient Hebrew might mention the "firmament" in his account, reflecting his primitive notion that one of the most important elements in the universe was this dome holding back the waters. A contemporary of Aristotle might mention the beautiful crystalline spheres that carried the planets around on their orbital paths. An inspired author in the age of Newton would praise the Creator for the infinity of the creation. A modern inspired author would incorporate the big bang into his or her creation account.

All these accounts would be communicating the same theological truth. But this truth would have to be extracted from the account by recognizing which elements of the account reflect the worldview of the author and which represent the profound truth that transcends that limited worldview.

If we presume to interpret the Genesis account of creation within the context of our modern worldview, we quickly find ourselves in an exegetical straitjacket, unable to maneuver through a literary maze of foreign concepts. We will be forced to acknowledge scientific error in the account, we will be forced to conclude that the words do not mean exactly what they say, and so on. As soon as we relax this a priori exegetical constraint, the account immediately makes perfect sense. No longer do we have to perform hermeneutical acrobatics to bring the primitive Hebrew concepts up to date. The Genesis account suddenly acquires a newfound clarity.

If we accept the dynamical theory of inspiration, then we are free to approach the Genesis account openly and without the uneasy feeling that some scientific concept will soon cast a shadow over its authority. It should be pointed out here that the dynamical theory of inspiration is finding acceptance within the evangelical church as scholars are coming to the realization that the approach of the fundamentalists is no longer tenable in light of recent scientific developments. While it is not as simple as the doctrine of plenary verbal inspiration embraced by the fundamentalists, scholars from many mainstream denominations accept the dynamical theory in some form.[6]

Furthermore, as we shall see in the next section, there is good reason to challenge the assumption that Genesis 1 is a scientific account and should be interpreted accordingly.

The Nature of the Genesis Account

The Bible contains many kinds of literature. It was written over the course of many centuries by many authors with many different individual purposes. Some passages are poetic and find themselves included in literature anthologies. Some passages teach wisdom, some teach ethics, some are history, some are geography, and so on. The Bible is not an organized dissertation on the Judeo-Christian tradition, written from a single perspective.

The questions we must ask, then, within the context of this discussion, are: What kind of literature is the first chapter of Genesis? In the original Hebrew does it read like a newspaper account, suggesting the author was communicating literal facts?—or does it read like a poem, suggesting the author was writing from a different literary perspective?

These questions are very complex and have been dealt with at great length elsewhere.[7] All that is appropriate here is a summary of some of the key conclusions that evangelical scholars have reached regarding the nature of the Genesis account. The interested reader is referred to any of the many excellent works on Genesis for a further discussion.

---

6. See, for example, Howard J. Van Till's *The Fourth Day: What the Bible and the Heavens Are Telling Us About the Creation* (Grand Rapids: Eerdmans Publishing Co., 1986) for a discussion from the perspective of a thinker in the Reformed tradition. Charles Hummel presents similar ideas in *The Galileo Connection.* Hummel is a former president of Barrington College and is currently working for InterVarsity in campus ministries.

7. See, for example, Henri Blocher, *In the Beginning* (Downers Grove, Ill.: InterVarsity Press, 1984); N. H. Ridderbos, *Is There a Conflict Between Genesis 1 and Natural Science?* (Grand Rapids: Wm. B. Eerdmans, 1957); Conrad Hyers, *The Meaning of Creation: Genesis and Modern Science* (Atlanta: John Knox Press, 1984). Both of the following references also contain helpful discussions of the Genesis account.

The Hymn of Creation

The Genesis account was probably written while the children of Israel were wandering in the wilderness. It may have been based on an oral tradition that had developed over the preceding centuries. The account was written for the Israelites who as yet had no Scriptures and no organized religion, having resided in the pagan Egyptian culture for centuries. There was a pressing need for the Israelites to identify the God who was leading them out of bondage as the Creator of the universe. They needed a theological unity to provide a focus for their worldview.

One of the key organizing principles at the heart of the developing Jewish religion was the notion of the Sabbath. The Bible spends a remarkable amount of time discussing the significance of the Sabbath. The creation account, with its grand sabbatical finale, was a meaningful way to unite the day-to-day existence of the Israelites with their Creator. Thus, the significance of the week of creation is not the creative activity of the first six days but rather the Sabbath that comes at the end. The Jews were certainly more interested in the divine ordination of their Sabbath than in the details of how and when the plants and animals were created. H. Ray Dunning puts it like this: "The structure of the account of the process of creation in Genesis 1 is clearly set forth to emphasize the theological truth that the Sabbath principle is grounded in the creative activity of God."[8]

In fact, the Scriptures contain virtually no additional references to any of the six days of creation outside Genesis 1. After the first chapter of Genesis, only the Sabbath receives any more attention, and that attention is considerable. Thus, it would seem the modern creationist movement is giving the six days of creation far more emphasis than the Jews and the biblical writers ever did, even though the account was written by them and for them. In emphasizing the six days of creation to the exclusion of the seventh day of rest, the creationists demonstrate the significance of hermeneutical considerations. Their assumption

---

8. Dunning, *Grace, Faith, and Holiness*, 237-38.

that the account is scientific in nature leads them to dwell on the supposedly scientific portions of the account, namely the processes described during the first six days. If we assume that the account serves a religious, rather than scientific, purpose, then we find ourselves focusing on the seventh day of rest.

Whatever additional functions the creation account was supposed to serve, it is generally agreed that grounding the Jewish Sabbath directly in the creation was very important. This essentially religious function perhaps explains why the creation account resembles a hymn. H. Orton Wiley in his *Christian Theology* has an excellent discussion of this dimension of the creation account: "The Book of Genesis opens with an inspired Psalm, sometimes known as the 'Hymn of Creation,' and sometimes as the 'Poem of the Dawn.'"[9]

The preceding analysis dealt with the function of the Genesis account. By determining the meaning that it had for its primary audience, we gain insight into what it was trying to communicate. Besides the function of the account, we must also consider the form. Certain forms of literature reveal something about the purposes of their authors. These literary considerations will provide additional reasons for treating the Genesis creation account as a hymn.

1. The passage contains a number of alliterations. This, of course, cannot be discovered in the English translation.

2. Repetition plays a prominent role; the sentence "And God saw that it was good" serves as a refrain, tying the various creative acts of God together. Phrases like "And it was so," "And God said," appear several times.

3. God's creative act is treated anthropomorphically. God "speaks," "sees," "moves," "breathes." These are clearly metaphors, familiar residents of the land of poetry. We know God does not do any of these things, for God is a Spirit, and these are the activities of a physical being. But literary license permits these colorful images.

4. The writer uses numbers 3, 7, and 10 in a very specific coherent way. The account starts with three elements to be

---

9. Wiley, *Christian Theology*, 1:449.

formed—earth, darkness, and watery deep. These are dealt with within two sets of three days. *Create* is used at three points. The phrase "and it was so" appears seven times, as does "God saw that it was good." The phrase "God said" appears 10 times, as does "make" and "according to its kind."[10]

5. There are places in the account where the words rhyme. As is the case with the alliterations, this is completely lost in the translation.

The elaborate internal structure of the account is more characteristic of poetry than narrative. No scientific literature ever uses these kinds of literary devices. If this account is contrasted with, say, the story of Abraham and Isaac, it becomes clear that it is a much different kind of literature. Furthermore, when the creation is discussed elsewhere in the Bible, it is absolutely clear that its literary form is poetry. Consider the following passage from Job 38:

Then the Lord answered Job out of the storm. He said . . .
"Where were you when I laid the earth's foundation?
    Tell me, if you understand.
Who marked off its dimensions? Surely you know!
    Who stretched a measuring line across it?
On what were its footings set,
    or who laid its cornerstone—
while the morning stars sang together
    and all the angels shouted for joy?
Who shut up the sea behind doors
    when it burst forth from the womb?
when I made the clouds its garment
    and wrapped it in thick darkness" (vv. 1, 4-9).

This account from Job is clearly poetic. Its references to the natural world are so colorful that we are not even tempted to go after this account with a scientific hermeneutic. In the same way, we must recognize that there is a similar strong poetic

---

10. For a truly excellent discussion of this topic see Charles Hummel's *The Galileo Connection*. Hummel shows how the original Hebrew text for Genesis divides up naturally into a series of eight poems, with repetitive endings and beginnings tying them all together into a pattern. Wiley's *Christian Theology* also does an excellent job of laying out the Genesis account in such a way as to clarify its literary character.

spirit in the first chapter of Genesis, although the colorful language is more restrained. Those who would make the Old Testament teach modern scientific theories of origins never refer us to this chapter in Job; neither should they refer us to the account of Genesis. Both accounts affirm powerful theological truths; neither are scientific.

Conclusion

There are many reasons why we should not require that modern science agree with the Genesis account of creation. Even the most conservative of scholars admit that there is considerable ambiguity in exactly what the first chapter of Genesis is trying to say. Those who take the account as literally true still have serious disagreements about its interpretation. And this has always been the case. Even though the authority of the Bible was not seriously challenged until fairly recently, no consensus ever developed within the Christian tradition as to what the Genesis account was trying to teach. To insist that there is a single unambiguous exegesis of this scripture is to ignore the entire history of the Christian Church.

The tremendous divergence of opinion on the meaning of Genesis, both current and historical, should, at the very least, dampen the enthusiasm of anyone who thinks his or her personal exegetical conclusions should become dogma. Furthermore, there are very serious *scientific* problems that emerge when the Bible is presumed to speak scientifically. These problems put the Bible at odds with much of modern science and should provide a powerful incentive for Christians to suspend judgment on the scientific significance of Genesis. At the same time, we must enthusiastically affirm its theological message.

9

The Emperor's New Science

• • • • •

*We should take all means to prevent such an
embarrassing situation, in which people
show up vast ignorance in a Christian and
laugh it to scorn.*

Augustine

• • • • •

From Canadian humorist Stephen Leacock's *Sunshine Sketches of
a Little Town*—

Mallory Tompkins was a young man with long legs
and checked trousers who worked on the *Mariposa Times-
Herald*. That was what gave him his literary taste. He
used to read Ibsen and that other Dutch author—Bum-
ston Bumstone, isn't it?—and you can judge that he was a
mighty intellectual fellow. He and Pupkin used to have
the most tremendous arguments about creation and evolution, and how if you study at a school of applied science you learn that there's no hell beyond the present life.

Mallory Tompkins used to prove absolutely that the
miracles were only electricity, and Pupkin used to admit
that it was an awfully good argument, but claimed that
he had heard it awfully well answered in a sermon,
though unfortunately he had forgotten how.

Tompkins used to show that the flood was contrary
to geology, and Pupkin would acknowledge that the
point was an excellent one, but that he had read a book—
the title of which he ought to have written down—which
explained geology away altogether.

Mallory Tompkins generally got the best of the
merely logical side of the arguments, but Pupkin—who

was a tremendous Christian—was much stronger in the things he had forgotten. So the discussions often lasted till far into the night, and Mr. Pupkin would fall asleep and dream of a splendid argument, which would have settled the whole controversy, only unfortunately he couldn't recall it in the morning.[1]

I Was a Teenage Fundamentalist

I grew up in the most wholesome of Christian families, in a community where traditional religious values were widely appreciated, and where ministers and priests were highly respected members of society. Traditional old-fashioned religious beliefs—Protestant and Catholic—were shared by almost everyone, and the evils of "secular humanism," "liberalism," and "evolutionism" were far away; nevertheless, I did encounter them in many of the fundamentalist books I so eagerly read. I decided I would dedicate my life to fighting against these various and sundry evils.

With this in mind, I began to read the books that told Christians how to defend their faith against these heresies. I studied fundamentalist theology and scientific creationism very carefully so that I could easily refute evolutionism, both scientifically and biblically. I even had some kind of a Greek Bible guide that would allow me to be a biblical scholar. Fundamentalist authors looked down approvingly from my bookshelf as I tried to make their arguments my own so that I might "always be prepared to give an answer to everyone who asks [me] to give the reason for the hope that [I] have" (1 Pet. 3:15).

Armed with this array of intellectual weaponry, I set out to join the battle on the front lines. I would go to college, get a Ph.D. in physics, and become a champion of scientific creationism. Following in the footsteps of my mentors, I would challenge the atheistic evolutionists to debate me in front of large audiences, and I would tear their feeble arguments to shreds, for I had the "truth." I practiced on everyone with whom I came in contact, a practice not universally appreciated.

---

1. Stephen Leacock, *Sunshine Sketches of a Little Town* (Salem, N.H.: Ayer Co. Publishers, 1991 reprint of 1912 original work), 160-61.

During my freshman year in college I had the opportunity to attend a creation seminar in a local church led by none other than Dr. Henry Morris himself. During an intermission we had a pleasant conversation, and he autographed my well-worn copy of his manifesto on Christian apologetics, *Many Infallible Proofs*. He also encouraged me in my pursuit of a Ph.D., which he said would be a valuable weapon in the war against evolution. I came away renewed in my enthusiasm and even more inspired to join this fine army of persecuted warriors, as they attempted to overthrow the devil-inspired scientific establishment.

But something happened en route to my Ph.D. I began to see that modern science was not the grand hoax the creationists said it was. In fact, I discovered that science was ruthlessly honest and that this honesty was at the very heart of the scientific process. True, there have been hoaxes perpetrated by individuals within the scientific community, but it was this community, policing itself in the interest of truth, that detected and exposed the hoaxes. I discovered that philosophical and religious considerations were not a part of the scientific method and that most scientists were quite incompetent in matters of philosophy and religion, which they perceived as irrelevant to their discipline.

Scientists working in laboratories, at computers, and in the field were, it seemed to me, gathering little bits of truth called facts, which they would then explain in the most logical way possible. Scientists seemed to pay absolutely no attention to the religious implications of their work. Try as I might, I could not find this coven of scientists huddled together in the back of the laboratory, conspiring to ensure that evolution continued its reign of unchallenged deception.

I discovered that the greatest accomplishment in all of science was to overthrow a well-established theory. The Nobel prize is awarded each year to the scientists who are the best at this; and probably two Nobel prizes would be awarded to anyone with ingenuity to overthrow such an important theory as evolution. So I began to question the "evolution as a scientific conspiracy to suppress the truth of creation" hypothesis that I had encountered in the many scientific creationism books that I had read.

I discovered that this conspiracy theory could not possibly be true. As I journeyed into the heart of the scientific enterprise and began to publish research results of my own, it became clear to me that it would be utterly impossible to organize the kind of grand-scale scientific deception the creationists claim evolution to be.

I learned that one of the primary tasks of the scientist is to identify problems with the existing explanations—to destroy the scientific bandwagon, not simply to jump on. I discovered that every single scientific experiment, no matter how trivial, had the potential to refute the grandest scheme of explanation; but no experiment was capable of confirming such explanation. I was astonished to learn that any time a remarkable result is achieved, numerous scientists all over the world repeated the experiment to see if they could disprove it. It seemed to me that the entire scientific community was very distrustful of itself. Nobody would ever just believe someone's results; they had to repeat the experiment for themselves, and possibly disprove the new result.

A much clearer picture of the scientific enterprise began to emerge during this time, one that was quite different from what I had expected to find, based on my creationist background. I found that the day-to-day practice of science was not affected in any way by the philosophical assumptions of the scientists. Science was like carpentry—it did not matter what your religious convictions were. Just as there was no such thing as a Christian way to build a house, so there was no such thing as a Christian way to do science. All that mattered was your competence. And there were thousands of scientists who all kept a close watch on each other to ensure that nobody could be incompetent and get away with it. It seemed the scientific community was very diligently searching for the "truth" and jealously guarded itself against making any unnecessary errors. The occasional incompetent or dishonest scientist was usually discovered and promptly drummed out of science.

As this new perspective on science crystallized, I began to reexamine the case for scientific creationism. I discovered that it was not as strong as I had originally thought. Arguments that looked quite solid to a college sophomore were not at all convincing to a physics Ph.D. Furthermore, my understanding of the nature of science made it clear to me that evolution could not possibly be based on the philosophical foundations of atheism, as the scientific creationists insisted. To make matters worse, many of the things I had studied in graduate school were not properly understood by the creationist scientists. But how could that be? I asked myself. Why is it that *I* can understand quantum mechanics, for example, but *they* cannot?

And then I made an astonishing discovery: The creationist experts were all writing outside their field! A biochemist was writing books on paleontology; a civil engineer was writing about nuclear physics; a high school teacher was writing about genetics—this was the problem with scientific creationism.[2]

I began to understand why none of the creationists were able to publish in regular scientific journals. Their claim about the evolution conspiracy sounded quite hollow when I realized that virtually none of them were doing research for which they were qualified and, in fact, they really weren't doing any kind of scientific research at all! I was dismayed to learn that the "Institute for Creation Research" had no better research facilities than a good high school. Their graduate school conferred master's degrees in my field (physics) for theses that were scientifically preposterous, such as "A Classical Field Theory for the Propagation of Light," which attempts to explain quantum phenomena using classical physics by invoking the long-discarded ether hypothesis that was totally discredited 75 years ago.[3]

---

2. Many doctorates held by well-known creation scientists are honorary or from schools lacking accreditation. See Volume 9, no. 6 (1989) of the "National Center for Science Education: Reports," 15-16, printed by the National Center for Science Education. (There is nothing wrong, of course, with honorary degrees. But it would seem that the creationists are so desperate to be taken seriously that they exaggerate their educational credentials.)

3. This is discussed in detail in the "California State Department of Education: Report of Visitation, January 12, 1990." This report comments that the master's degree in question was considered unacceptable by the dean of ICR but was accepted out of "courtesy for Professor Barnes and consideration of the time and effort that the student

Instead of actually doing research, the institute's staff were spending their time and money to produce literature that gives the false impression that a massive ground swell of discontent existed within the scientific community about their major theories. They seemed unaware that science was a communal activity based on consensus. There are always people, even competent people, around the fringes who do not agree with the conclusions of the mainstream. When attention is focused exclusively on these fringe perspectives, as the creationists like to do, then it is easy to conclude erroneously that many scientific theories, such as evolution, are in disarray. The reality is that there are actually very few scientists who disagree with the science *within their area of expertise.* It is one thing for a biochemist to challenge the standard interpretation of the fossil record; biochemists don't know all that much about fossils. It is quite another for a paleontologist, professionally trained in that area, to challenge that fossil record.

As I penetrated deeper and deeper into the heart of my chosen discipline of physics, I grew to understand how complicated a scientific theory can be. I struggled mightily to understand quantum mechanics, both in the ethereal world of the textbook where the language was mathematical, and then in the laboratory where the language was experimental. I began to appreciate the incredible effort that had gone into unraveling this manifestation of God's creation, the untold efforts by the greatest minds of my discipline—Einstein, Heisenberg, Feynman, Bohr. And I became dismayed at its casual dismissal by creationists who had not invested this same effort in understanding it.

I began to understand why there was only one geology Ph.D. in the entire country who accepted the flood geology explanation, which had been proposed by nongeologists. Could it be that if you really understand geology, then you know that creationist geology cannot be correct?

---

had put into it," not the usual criteria for the evaluation of a master's thesis. The report goes on to consider almost all of the master's degrees awarded by ICR and concludes that, for the most part, they are sadly deficient and would not have been accepted at other institutions.

Eventually I came to realize that this whole question was not one of science. This big debate over origins is not like the debate in astronomy over the origin of the planet Pluto, in which there are several scientific explanations, all of which are legitimate and all of which have competent adherents. No, the issue of creation science is not a scientific question at all; if it were, it would be debated in the scientific press—and it is not. When the creationists tried to get their views into the Arkansas educational curriculum, the judge ruled, after careful consideration and much expert testimony, that scientific creationism simply was not science. In fact, many philosophers of science have carefully examined the claims of creationism and discovered that it simply cannot be considered a science.

So I concluded that if I wanted to be a scientist, I could not be a creation scientist. I could still believe that "in the beginning God created the heavens and the earth." I could still affirm the theological truths that I had learned at my mother's knee. But I could no longer presume that the scientific creationists had figured out just how God had accomplished this wondrous event.

What Is a Science?

Creationism is not a science, because it does not meet the standard criteria of science. Any discipline claiming to be a science must be capable of doing the following: (1) making predictions that can be tested and either confirmed or refuted by the observations and measurements that result from those tests; (2) discarding or modifying its theories if the hypotheses are not verified by observations and measurements. A fundamental requirement of science as it is normally practiced is that it must present its conclusions to the scientific community so that they can try to falsify the theory. That's why scientists are so eager to refute any and all scientific theories (especially if those theories were proposed by someone else!). If the theory cannot present falsifiable predictions, then it cannot be a scientific theory.

The central question about creation science is not really whether it is right or wrong, although that is certainly an issue that can be debated. The question is rather "Is creationism a science?" The problem is compounded by the fact that questions of origins lie at the very edge of science, at the boundary be-tween science and metaphysics. Science can certainly address questions about the origin of a mountain, a river, or even the earth itself. But questions about the ultimate origin of matter and energy are more ambiguous.[4] And ambiguity generates conflict.

This volatile issue is simply one of authority. The creation-ists believe science has no authority to investigate origins. They believe theories of origins must be based on the Bible. That is why scientific qualification is not a relevant factor in their pre-sentation. That is why they think it is inappropriate to listen to the views of "unbelieving scientists." They believe radioactive dating is all wrong because it disagrees with the Bible. It does not require a Ph.D. in physics to come to that conclusion. They believe transitional fossils can't exist because "the Bible tells them so." Again, it does not require a degree in paleontology to come to that conclusion. And so on down the line: The scientific creationists are like students taking a true-and-false test when they have the answer key already. They don't have to know anything or even read the question to mark the correct answer. They already have it.

The Clothes of the Emperor

In this chapter we will look briefly at some of the scientific problems with the creationist arguments. We will not analyze them in any detail but simply point out the kinds of scientific errors that arise when we force the Genesis account of creation to be a scientific document. The reader is referred to the grow-ing literature emerging from the scientific community for more information on the status of creation science.

---

4. Some of the questions being pondered now in particle physics and cosmology are getting extremely close to what can legitimately be called *ultimate*. There have been proposals by prominent physicists that the universe originated out of nothing in a bizarre process known as a vacuum fluctuation. This process involves the production of a universe out of the instabilities inherent in the quantum mechanical vacuum, which is as close to a vacuum as physical theories predict you can get. The reason why there is something, rather than nothing, is that *nothing* is unstable. In the irreverent words of MIT physicist Alan Guth, the originator of this idea, "The universe is the ultimate free lunch."

Arguments from Physics

1. The creationists' favorite argument is based on the famous (and now, perhaps, infamous) second law of thermodynamics, which states that there is a universal tendency in nature for things to proceed to ever-simpler arrangements.[5] Statues disintegrate, people die, paint fades, and so on. Things naturally run downhill, toward disorganization, which is the opposite of evolution. The law has a very precise mathematical form, but the creationists generally prefer the "layman's version," since it is hard to apply the mathematical form to biological systems. "The evolutionary process is completely precluded by the Second Law of Thermodynamics. There seems no way of modifying the basic evolutionary model to accommodate this Second Law."[6]

This application of the second law is totally invalid however. The second law applies only to hypothetical "closed" systems, which are systems that do not interact with any energy source outside of themselves. And living systems, by definition, are very interactive with external energy sources. There are, in fact, no completely closed systems in nature (except the universe, considered as a single system), and the second law is useful only to the extent that the system under consideration approximates a closed system. Any time a system experiences an external interaction with an energy source, there can occur numerous *apparent* violations of the second law, in which order within that system appears to emerge spontaneously and remarkably from disorder.

For example, when the sun shines on certain molecules, they combine into larger and more complex molecules appearing, it would seem, to mysteriously violate the second law. This is the basis of photosynthesis. If you dissolve salt in water and then leave it alone for a while, very ordered crystals will appear

---

5. Precisely stated, the second law reads (in one of several equivalent formulations), "The Entropy Inventory of the World Tends to a Maximum." This statement is from Clausius, the thermodynamicist who coined the word *entropy* to refer to the amount of unusable energy contained in a system, and was written in 1865. Stated mathematically, the law has a very precise form that is difficult to apply to biological systems in the way the creationists like to do.

6. Morris, *Scientific Creationism*, 45.

in the container, in apparent violation of the second law. The rock candy sold in candy stores originates in a "thermodynamically impossible" sugar crystallization. The formation of snowflakes requires the production of order from disorder. As another example, the waves on a beach organize the small stones along the beach so that the large ones are closer to the water than the small ones. An initially random organization of stones on a beach will become organized by the sorting action of the waves. A disordered box of corn flakes will order itself through a simple shaking.

There are countless examples of natural phenomena in which we find order naturally arising from disorder. These various examples demonstrate that many phenomena considered in isolation do not obey the second law.

An adequate understanding of the second law of thermodynamics clearly reveals that it poses no barrier to evolution. This is not to say that evolution is true or that the second law supports it (it does not), but only that people who argue that it is a barrier to evolution do not understand it or are misusing it.[7] The creationists could argue, with exactly the same validity, that the formation of snowflakes is impossible.

2. Creationists like to argue that radioactive decay rates are not valid indicators of age. Their arguments here are based on the fact that radioactively determined ages for the earth give a number in billions of years, not thousands, as they insist the Bible teaches. Radioactivity is one of the best understood phenomenon in physics; it is so straightforward that students in introductory physics courses frequently encounter it in their laboratory exercises. There is a very comprehensive theory that explains how it works, and there are an unlimited number of experimental verifications of the theory.

One common dating process is known as carbon 14 dating. It can be understood as follows: your body has a lot of carbon in it. This carbon came from plants that got it from the atmosphere by plant breathing. There are a number of different forms of car-

---

7. Philosopher of science Philip Kitcher has an excellent discussion of the creationists' misuse of the second law of thermodynamics. See *Abusing Science: The Case Against Creationism* (Cambridge, Mass.: MIT Press, 1982), 89-96.

bon in the atmosphere; the two kinds of carbon in the atmosphere of particular interest in this context are carbon 12 and carbon 14. (The number indicates the number of particles in the nucleus.) These two forms of carbon are present in a fixed ratio in the atmosphere. The plants acquire them in this ratio, and thus you digest them in this ratio when you eat plants (or animals that ate plants). This fixed ratio is like the ratio of hydrogen to oxygen in water. Whatever water you have in you, there will be two atoms of hydrogen for each of oxygen.

Unlike the ratio of hydrogen to oxygen in water, the ratio of carbon 14 to carbon 12 does not remain constant after one dies. Over a period of 5,700 years, about half of the carbon 14 will change into nitrogen 14, under the relentless prodding of the weak nuclear force. The ratio will thus change over time. Initially the ratio will be the same in the organism as it is in the atmosphere, but the ratio will gradually decline as the carbon 14 disappears but the carbon 12 remains the same (it is not radioactive). Thus, a determination of the ratio can yield the age of the organism. This method of dating is extremely accurate and has been vindicated many times by dating things of known age (such as an object or a body from a known period in history). It was recently used to date the shroud of Turin and showed that it was from the late Middle Ages and thus could not be the burial cloth of Jesus.

Radioactive dating is absolutely trustworthy.[8] It involves the steady decay of the nucleus, one of the most constant processes in nature. There are no known normal external influences like temperature, humidity, or magnetic fields that can change the decay rate. The creationists, however, disagree: "Every process in nature operates at a rate which is influenced by a number of different factors. If any of these factors change, the process rate changes. Rates are at best only statistical averages, not deterministic constants."[9]

---

8. Radioactive dating, while very simple and straightforward theoretically, can be very complex in practice. The determination of a date radioactively requires very precise measurements on a very well chosen sample of uncontaminated material. It is thus possible for different laboratories to obtain somewhat different ages for the same object. On average, however, competent laboratories will come up with similar ages.

9. Morris, *Scientific Creationism*, 139.

This last sentence is typical of the kind of misleading statements made by the creationists. To dismiss something because it is only a statistical average betrays either complete ignorance of statistics or a deliberate attempt to mislead the uninformed. In fact, the most useful information that we possess about our world is based on statistical averages. Should we dismiss the following numbers as invalid, unreliable, or irrelevant because they are only statistical averages: (1) the nine-month gestation period for a fetus; (2) the rate of population growth in the last decade; (3) the number of cells in a human body; (4) the average income of a college professor? Are all these numbers meaningless because they are statistical?

Furthermore, the "different factors" that are proposed to affect this rate are ludicrous. One suggested factor is supernovas, which are so rare and insignificant as to be irrelevant. (Written history records only a handful of supernovas.) Furthermore, the creationists do not propose any mechanism by which supernovas might affect the steady decay of radioactive materials or whether the effect would tend to increase or decrease the apparent age being estimated. (Even if supernovas were relevant, they could not affect the decay rate—only the configuration of the decaying nucleus.)

The only plausible relevant factors that could affect the rate of radioactive decay of the nucleus would have to include (1) the detailed properties of the nuclear particles (their mass, charge, composition) and (2) the precise nature of the physical forces that describe their interactions. It would be an extraordinary scientific accomplishment indeed to show how any of these might have changed in such a way as to affect the process of radioactive decay.

Elementary knowledge of radioactivity reveals the creationists' arguments to be without scientific foundation. Unfortunately, much of this literature is written for people without such knowledge, people who are likely to be misled by confident assertions that radioactive dating is invalid.

3. Other arguments from physics demonstrate that the creationists do not understand the big bang theory, the way light travels in the universe, planetary magnetic fields, the origin of

comets, and so on. They dispute the big bang theory, claiming there is "not a shred of evidence to prove it,"[10] when every high school astronomy book in the country lists several very significant evidences that cannot be adequately explained by any of the alternative theories. They also like to point out that "none of the evolutionists were there to see the big bang,"[11] as if that is some kind of meaningful objection. They appeal to obscure and irrelevant papers to find some way for light to get across the universe in less than the billions of years it clearly requires[12]; they claim to be able to calculate the age of the earth from the decay of the earth's magnetic field,[13] one of the most poorly understood phenomenon in all of geology and far less reliable than radioactive dating, which they dismiss. And so on down the list. They are so convinced they have the answer before they even investigate the phenomenon that they jump to all kinds of careless conclusions.

Arguments from Biology

4. Another favorite argument of the creationists is that there are "systematic gaps in the fossil record"[14] and a complete absence of transitional forms. The argument is that the fossil record supports the creationists' claim that a system of biological classification can be accomplished based on the *kinds* described in Genesis. This is simply not true, however, and the creationists have not been able to determine what a kind is, even though it is one of the key pillars of their case. And while it is true that there are a large number of presently unexplained gaps in the fossil record, they do not occur where the creation-

---

10. Harold Slusher, *Clues Regarding the Ages of the Universe,* reprinted in *The Battle for Creation,* ed. Henry Morris and Duane T. Gish (San Diego: Creation-Life Publishers, 1976), 253.

11. Ken Ham, "The Big Bang Is Coming," *Back to Genesis* (June 1990). Printed by the Institute for Creation Research, El Cajon, Calif.

12. Harold Slusher, *Age of the Cosmos* (San Diego: Institute for Creation Research, 1980), 33.

13. Henry Morris et al., *Science, Scripture and the Young Earth* (El Cajon, Calif.: Institute for Creation Research, 1989), 52. This book is a personal attack on geologist Davis Young of Calvin College, whose writings in defense of modern science have been very influential among Evangelicals.

14. Morris, *Scientific Creationism,* 78.

ists need them most. For example, there are no gaps between the two broadest classes of living organisms—plant and animal. There are so many intermediate forms along the continuum between plant and animal that it is impossible to classify the organisms as either plant or animal.[15] Surely there should be a systematic gap here, of all places.

5. Creationists like to claim that "the net effect of mutations is harmful."[16] A mutation is an error in the genetic code of the organism. It causes that organism to be a little bit different from its peers and, frequently but not always, this difference is harmful to the organism. But it does increase the variety—and thus the potential for adaptation—in the gene pool of the species, and this is beneficial to the species, even though it may not be beneficial for that particular organism.

Evolution claims that a long series of mutations can lead to a different organism, although the details of this process are not yet understood. Even though the mechanics of the transition from one species to another is not well understood, numerous experiments have been done on many different organisms and have clearly demonstrated that mutations *can* be very beneficial to the organism.[17] The ability of insects to resist formerly toxic chemicals is the result of lifesaving mutations.

6. There are numerous other arguments that clearly indicate that the creationists either do not understand biology very well or are deliberately attempting to mislead their readers. We will only consider one more here: their claim that natural selection is "incapable of either test or proof."[18] This is a totally false claim refuted by numerous examples, including the one above involving pesticide-resistant insects. In particular, the ever-popular fruit flies have been subjected to a variety of experiments in which natural selection was shown to preserve those flies that had certain beneficial mutations.

---

15. Chris McGowan, *In the Beginning . . . A Scientist Shows Why the Creationists Are Wrong* (Buffalo, N.Y.: Prometheus Books, 1984), 69.
16. Morris, *Scientific Creationism*, 56.
17. Douglas J. Futuyma, *Science on Trial* (New York: Pantheon Books, 1983), 132-47.
18. Duane T. Gish, "Cracks in the Neo-Darwinian Jericho," in *Impact* (December 1976), i. Printed by the Institute for Creation Research, El Cajon, Calif.

Natural selection is very complicated, and it is hard to design experiments to study it. The main reason is that the scope of the experiments is far beyond that of the laboratory. It is simply not possible to bring an entire species of dogs into the lab and observe them for a hundred generations and watch natural selection at work. So biologists are constrained to study much more humble animals, like the fruit fly, and then try to extrapolate from the small to the large.

Arguments from Biochemistry

7. "It seems beyond all question that such complex systems as the DNA molecule could never arise by chance, no matter how big the universe nor how long is time."[19] DNA is deoxyribonucleic acid, which is so hard to pronounce that we call it simply DNA. It is a special molecular structure that carries the genetic information of an organism. It is very complicated, so complicated that the creationists claim there is absolutely no way it could ever evolve from simpler chemicals. But the truth is that experiments have demonstrated that simplified versions of DNA can be produced in experiments and then observed to actually evolve. Biologist Douglas J. Futuyma states this clearly in his book *Science on Trial:* "Under conditions resembling those on the prebiotic earth, simple organic molecules actually form from elementary constituents (ammonia, methane, etc.) and assemble themselves into self-replicating nucleic acids which mutate and are altered in frequency by natural selection, all in the laboratory."[20]

At the time that he wrote these words, Futuyma was quite optimistic about the possibility of producing life in the laboratory; he went on to predict that simple life forms would be produced in the laboratory within 10 years of the time he wrote the above. Those 10 years have now passed, and the origin of life is, if anything, an even bigger mystery. But there are a number of relevant scientific hypotheses currently under investigation to see whether any of them might be the code that deciphers the

19. Futuyma, *Science on Trial,* 62.
20. Ibid., 223.

riddle of the origin of life. In all cases, the scenarios successfully explain the origin of extremely complex chemical systems, in apparent violation of the second law of thermodynamics, that are legitimate intermediates between nonliving and living systems.[21]

There are countless additional arguments that could be elaborated here. The reader is referred back to note 17 of this chapter for a source listing 28 separate invalid creationist arguments. It is a testimony to the growing popularity of the creationist movement that so many books are being written now discussing their use and misuse of science.

So What?

There are two reasons why we must be wary of the scientific dimensions of creationism.

1. Creation science is not always good science, as we summarized in the above analysis of some of their key arguments. Evangelical scholars Howard J. Van Till, Clarence Menninga, and Davis Young have analyzed the scientific method as it is applied by the creationists. They present their conclusions in their book *Science Held Hostage*, in which they demonstrate distinct cases in which the creationists have displayed utter disregard for the standard procedures of science, thus diminishing their credibility as scientific authorities, which they so desperately want to maintain. "A commitment to the 'scientific creationist' picture of cosmic history has functioned to diminish the demand for both craft competence and professional integrity and to disable the generally accepted epistemic value system. *When natural science is held hostage to support preconceived answers, it can no longer serve in the open-minded search for knowledge.*"[22]

---

21. See, for example, John Horgan, "In the Beginning . . ." in *Scientific American* (February 1991), 117, for an excellent summary of the current efforts to explain the origin of life. While it is clear that the problem is a long way from solution, and may even require some approach radically different from those employed at present, it is very dangerous to go out on a limb and say that there will *never* be a scientific explanation for the origin of life. Understanding the origin of life is more complex than understanding the origin of the universe. It may very well take a century to solve that scientific riddle.

22. Howard J. Van Till et al., *Science Held Hostage* (Downers Grove: InterVarsity Press, 1988), 45, emphasis added.

One of the examples the authors of *Science Held Hostage* analyze in detail is the creationists' use of moon dust as an evidence for a young solar system. By misusing some data and disregarding others, the creationists were able to claim that the actual thickness of dust on the moon was far less than that predicted on the basis of the standard theories for the age of the moon. But their use of the data betrayed the same carelessness that gave rise to the long list above. The authors concluded:

> The claim that a thick layer of dust should be expected on the surface of the moon, and the claim that not more than a few inches of dust were found on the surface of the moon, are contradicted by an abundance of published evidence. The continuing publication of those claims by young-earth advocates constitutes an intolerable violation of the standards of professional integrity that should characterize the work of natural scientists.[23]

2. Creation science is making many God of the gaps arguments. This is an uncertain road, full of pitfalls, and one that has always led to embarrassment in the past. The creationists are quite correct in pointing out that science does not have a very satisfactory explanation for *(a)* the origin of life, *(b)* the mechanism by which one species undergoes a macroevolutionary (large-scale) change into another species, *(c)* the formation of stars and galaxies, *(d)* the source of the earth's magnetic field, and so on. There are certainly many important questions in science, which is why it continues to attract curious people to its various disciplines. But it is dangerous to assume that all these as yet undiscovered pathways lead directly to God. We must remember that gap theology died in the previous century, and it probably cannot be resurrected to solve the mysteries of contemporary evolutionary theory. The faith of the scientist is that the mysteries have solutions; the methods of science are the rules that govern the hunt for those solutions.

The creationists have, however, served a very useful function in pointing out the exaggerated claims of the scientific community as they have sometimes presented their theories as if all of the details were already worked out. It is certainly legitimate

---

23. Ibid., 82.

to insist that any problems with scientific theories be presented as such. Good scientific literature takes great pains to communicate any serious difficulties with a theory. A recent summary of the various origin of life hypotheses started out with a straightforward acknowledgment of ignorance: "Scientists are having a hard time agreeing on when, where, and—most important— how life first emerged on the earth."[24] Careful scientists, when they are speaking as such, make it clear when there is uncertainty in the theories.

As a physicist, for example, I find it very interesting, and mildly unsettling, that something as basic as the formation of stars is still unexplained within the context of the big bang theory of cosmology. I therefore consider it inappropriate for scientists to talk about the big bang in the same way that we might talk about the atom, for example. Atomic theory is fully worked out; there are no deep scientific mysteries (although there are certainly philosophical ones), and universal agreement within the scientific community has been achieved on this theory.

This is not the case, however, with the big bang. While there are many good reasons to believe the big bang theory is correct, it does not now enjoy the status of atomic theory. Eventually the big bang will have to accommodate a plausible mechanism for the formation of stars if it is to maintain its broad acceptance. If the big bang fails to do this within a reasonable period of time, it may very well be supplanted by another theory, which is better able to explain various phenomena associated with cosmology. This is the way of science.[25]

There are many deep problems with evolution, as the creationists have pointed out. But it is a complicated theory with

---

24. See reference 21.

25. As this book was going to press, astronomers announced that they had discovered irregularities in the radiation pattern from the big bang. It is believed these irregularities are probably the cosmic seeds from which the stars and galaxies formed, although the details have not yet been worked out. In any event, the discovery provided important additional confirmation of the big bang theory and removed some, if not most, of the mystery about the formation of the stars and galaxies. This is a remarkable example of science at its best—experimentalists gathering careful observational data that will either enhance or diminish the credibility of a theory. One of the most serious problems with the big bang theory, and the one to which I referred in the paragraphs above, has now been resolved. See Corey S. Powell, "The Golden Age of Cosmology," *Scientific American* (July 1992), 17.

many facets. It has been very successful in organizing the vast data of biology into a coherent whole. It has done an excellent job explaining the geographical distribution of animals; it can, for example, explain why there are so many odd-looking animals on the continent of Australia. Small-scale evolution (microevolution) has been demonstrated in the laboratory and is very well understood and widely accepted, even by the creationists. But many problems, such as the explanation of macroevolution and the origin of life, persist. Evolutionary theory will eventually have to answer these questions, or it, like Aristotle's crystalline spheres, will have to yield to another, better theory.

In the meantime, we must be careful that we do not dwell on the deficiencies of any particular scientific theory, conclude that it is totally wrong because it cannot deal with all of the problems, and then embrace a theological explanation in its place. Theories in science are accepted, not because they can explain everything and have no problems, but because they can explain much and have fewer problems than alternative theories. It is in the very nature of a scientific theory that it be open to further improvement, supplementation, or even replacement. Scientific knowledge is always expanding. This stream of new information provides a constant source of evaluation for existing theories.

In some cases, like quantum theory, every single new piece of information has confirmed the theory in all of its details, leading to its universal acceptance today. In other cases, like the big bang theory, the evidence has been primarily, but not universally, supportive, leading to the current uneasy feeling among cosmologists that there is something important missing at present. In the case of the origin of life, the stream of new information has not led anywhere, and confusion, which is a powerful impetus for science, has been the result.

There was a time when the sun-centered, moving-earth, Copernican cosmology had serious problems. Renaissance theologians, and even scientists, could refuse to accept it because there were problems with it, phenomena that it could not explain. But it became accepted, not because it could explain everything, but because it did such a good job of explaining many things. Eventually, of course, the problems were solved and it achieved universal acceptance.

There is a battle going on now. The battle is over authority in matters of origins. We can choose to ignore the lessons of history and build our science on the Book of Genesis. We can bring the contemporary Galileos[26] before our religious inquisitions and insist that they recant whatever scientific ideas they have that might happen to disagree with the Bible. We can wrap the gospel of Jesus Christ up in pseudoscience and fuzzy rhetoric and then exclaim about how modern science is so antagonistic toward that gospel. We can ignore the extraordinary benefits that science has bestowed on humanity, from modern medicine to beautiful pictures of Saturn, and claim that science is just a conspiracy to destroy faith in God. We can withdraw into the cozy confines of our stained-glass cathedrals with their motifs from the Middle Ages and try to believe that those motifs have not changed. We can certainly do all of this. It is our privilege. But at what price?

Can the Church of Jesus Christ afford to divorce itself from modern science? Can we circle our wagons around a particular theory of origins and defend that theory against all attacks, no matter what the source?

Modern culture is a tremendous force. It affects all classes of society. It affects the ignorant as well as the learned. What is to be done about it? In the first place the Church may simply withdraw from the conflict. She may simply allow the mighty stream of modern thought to flow by unheeded and do her work merely in the back-eddies of the current. There are still some men in the world who have been unaffected by modern culture. They may still be won for Christ without intellectual la-

---

26. The Christian Reformed Church recently put Howard J. Van Till, Clarence Menninga, and Davis Young (see reference 22) on "trial" for heresy. (The three suspected heretics were all faculty members at Calvin College, which is supported by the church.) The church convened a "Committee on Creation and Science" and evaluated their orthodoxy. The committee, to its credit, concluded that their writings "fall within the limits set by the synodically adopted guidelines for the interpretation of Scripture and by the doctrinal statements of the Christian Reformed Church; but, at the same time, the Board reminds the professors of the limitations that these guidelines place upon the interpretation of Scripture."

bor. And they must be won . . . If the Church is satisfied with that alone let her give up the scientific education of her ministry. Let her assume the truth of her message . . . Let her abandon the scientific study of history to the men of the world. In a day of increased scientific interest, let the Church go on becoming less scientific . . . By doing so she will win a straggler here and there. But her winnings will be but temporary. The great current of modern culture will sooner or later engulf her puny eddy. God will save her somehow—out of the depths. But the labor of centuries will have been swept away.[27]

These words were spoken in 1912 at the beginning of Princeton Seminary's second century by J. Gresham Machen, a great foe of the liberalism that was then challenging the Church. He recognized that the challenge of the Church was to stand firm on the fundamental truths of the gospel, but not to do so with eyes and ears closed to modern science.

Today the Church has the same challenge. The gospel of Jesus Christ must be defended against attack. The doctrine of God as Creator must be affirmed and reaffirmed, even as the understanding of that creation is being altered by advances in science. The "faith . . . once delivered unto the saints" (Jude 3, KJV) must be preserved. But this can be done only by confidently embracing modern science and making its universe into the one God created in Genesis, not the other way around. We must not allow the Church to wander back into the past, in search of the home where it lived as a child, before its worldview was forced to mature.

---

27. J. Gresham Machen, *Christianity and Culture,* quoted by Davis A. Young in "Theology and Natural Science," *The Reformed Journal* (May 1988), 12.

10

The Nature of Explanation

. . . . .

One of the most powerful human motivations is the need we feel to make sense of our experience, to gain a coherent and satisfying understanding of the world in which we live. It is a quest which unites science and theology in comradely concern, for they are both attempting to explore aspects of the way things are.

John Polkinghorne, former theoretical physicist,
now an Anglican priest

. . . . .

Student: Why is the sky blue? Is it because God made it blue?

Scientist: No. It's because the atmosphere scatters blue light more effectively than red light, making it appear that there is blue light coming from all parts of the atmosphere.

Student: Why does that happen?

Scientist: Because blue light is more energetic than red light.

Student: Why is that?

Scientist: Because blue light has a higher frequency and the energy is related to the frequency.

Student: Why does blue light have a higher frequency?

Scientist: Because blue light is produced from a more energetic process than red light.

Student: Why is that?

Scientist: Because of the details inherent in the laws of quantum mechanics.

Student: Why are the laws of quantum mechanics the way they are?

Scientist: Because very early in the history of the universe the laws of quantum mechanics developed from a prior condition in which all the physical laws were a part of one larger symmetrical configuration, a symmetry that disintegrated as the universe cooled from its initial hot state. The precise details of this disintegration, not all of which are understood at present, gave us our various different laws, including the laws of quantum mechanics.

Student: This is getting complex. What determined the conditions that were present at the very early stages of the evolution of the universe when the details of quantum mechanics were being determined?

Scientist: I have no idea. It is possible that they just emerged randomly from a potentiality latent in the vacuum. But science does not yet have an adequate understanding of the conditions at the very beginning of time.

Student: You sound very uncertain. Assuming this to be true, why did the "vacuum" have this latent potentiality?

Scientist: Our theories predict that all vacuums have a latent potentiality for the temporary creation of matter.

Student: How can matter come from the nothingness of a vacuum, even temporarily?

Scientist: This is described mathematically by the uncertainty principle of quantum mechanics, one of the most important concepts in modern physics.

Student: Where did the uncertainty principle come from?

Scientist: It came from the conditions at the beginning of the universe—the same conditions that determined the nature of all the forces.

Student: Did God establish the conditions at the beginning of the universe?

Scientist: I have no idea.

Student: Why do you have no idea about whether God established the conditions?

Scientist: Because our theories don't tell us about God. They tell us only about the physical universe. As a scientist I have absolutely no way to determine what exactly is due to the work of God. To answer such a question I would have to step outside the bounds of science and become a theologian; I would never want to do that.

Student: I would also prefer that you didn't do that.

Outline

In this chapter we will consider the nature of explanation. We will argue that scientific explanations are concerned primarily with the determination of cause and effect, while theological explanations are concerned primarily with questions of purpose. That there can be such divergent types of explanations for the same phenomenon has been recognized for some time. In fact, it was Aristotle who first identified the various types of explanation relevant to a phenomenon under examination.

In the second half of the chapter we will introduce the anthropic principle, an extraordinary hypothesis that seems to suggest that the laws of physics have their very detailed properties determined by the condition that life must be able to exist in the universe described by those laws. The anthropic principle represents an important point of contact for science and religion, as it cannot be understood without consideration of its scientific dimensions and it cannot be explained without consideration of its religious dimensions.

At the end of the chapter we will briefly consider the views of some contemporary thinkers who are enthusiastic about the potential for a fruitful dialogue between science and religion.

The Methods of Science

The conversation at the beginning of this chapter demonstrates the inability of science to provide truly ultimate answers. Eventually, all the scientist can do is throw up his or her hands and say, "That is the best I can do. The methods of my discipline do not allow me to proceed any further with the explanation." At some point in the quest for understanding, the scientific method becomes inadequate; it cannot provide any more information. In certain instances this breakdown occurs exactly at the point at which theology or philosophy become relevant.

Much of the current concern over the apparent incompatibility of science and religion relates to a misunderstanding of the methods of science: Just how does science go about its business? Does science ever arrive at a certain conclusion? Why is it that well-established scientific theories are occasionally overthrown? Are scientific ideas destined to be constantly revised, like a meandering stream that is never twice the same? How can religion, which seems to perceive its truths as immutable, get along with a science that seems to insist on the tentative nature of its conclusions?

These are difficult questions that cannot be resolved to everyone's satisfaction. It is agreed, however, that the enterprise of science is concerned not so much with the results or conclusions of any particular line of inquiry, but with the process by which nature, as experienced through observation and experiment, can be understood as completely as possible. To understand something according to modern science means to provide an explanation for it in terms of cause and effect.[1] We understand the tides by noting the effects of the gravity of the moon on the earth. We understand the decay of the nucleus by noting the effects of the weak nuclear force on the particles in the nucleus. We understand the action of a laser by noting the effects of the emission of light on other atoms.

Science seeks satisfactory explanations for natural phenomena. In this quest the scientist is simply responding to the innate curiosity we all share. For the scientist, however, a truly satisfactory explanation is an elusive quarry, for every answer raises another question, sometimes more than one. And at the end of the long quest for explanation is a door with a question like "Why does the universe exist?" written on it—a door science has no idea how to open. Thus, at the end of the long hallway of scientific explanation lies a door that can be opened only by a philosopher or a theologian, and then only in very specialized instances.

---

1. Modern physics has identified a number of phenomena that do not follow the classical laws of cause and effect. It is impossible, for example, to determine the cause of a radioactive disintegration because the process is somewhat random, and the order that exists is statistical. But science can discover the statistical laws and apply them to large ensembles.

It is the goal of science to open as many doors as possible before conceding (reluctantly) the investigation to the theologians.[2]

Recognizing the difference between the methods of science and religion is at the very heart of resolving the conflicts that exist over the issues of creation and evolution. A careful examination will reveal that creation is a theological concept and should be studied with the methods of theology; evolution, on the other hand, is a scientific concept, to be studied with the methods of science. They cannot be in conflict because they do not address the same portion of reality. Creation and evolution are thus *not* competing explanations for the same phenomenon; they are, rather, two levels of explanation that complement each other by providing the most general explanation possible for the phenomenon.

To consider this further, we will examine a relatively straightforward search for an explanation, one that does not entail any complicated ideas from theoretical physics, or emotion-laden ideas from the controversy over origins.

The Mystery of the Blank Page

Suppose, as you were reading this book, you discovered the page following this one was blank. That would probably strike you as odd, and you would be curious. "I wonder why this page is blank," you might say to yourself. You would have recognized that this was unusual and irregular and needed an explanation. This is the beginning of the scientific enterprise—the identification of a problem.

Now what would constitute a suitable explanation—one that would satisfy your curiosity about the blank page? Would you be satisfied with "the page has no ink on it"? Certainly not, even though this is actually a correct and relevant observation about the page. What about "the publisher decided to leave that page blank"? This would still be unsatisfactory, because this ex-

---

2. The "Vacuum Genesis" hypothesis is an attempt to provide an explanation for the origin of the universe that is without any philosophical or theological dimension. This speculative hypothesis suggests that what we call "nothing" is unstable and will erupt into raw material out of which a universe could emerge. While this is not entirely implausible it still fails to explain why "nothing"—a questionable label for something with the potential to make a universe—has this remarkable property.

planation does nothing but change the question from one about the page to one about the publisher. This kind of explanation would require that you consider questions of purpose—in the larger scheme of things, why did the publisher feel the need to leave this page blank?

At the point where it becomes necessary to consider purpose, a cloud has descended on the whole process. The explanation you seek, if it requires the discovery of a purpose that may exist in the mind of some individual who may not be available, or willing to talk to you, or even honest about his or her motivations, cannot be discovered with the standard techniques of science. A scientist you consulted would inform you that he or she was unable to help you discern this hidden purpose.

If you wrote to the publisher and asked for an explanation, the reply might be "our mechanical printer had a problem with that page due to a defective counter, and we did not discover the problem until all the books had been printed." You might feel satisfied at this point that you have an adequate explanation for the blank page. It would be a subjective judgment, however, as to whether you considered the explanation to be complete. You might feel that you don't really understand what the problem was with the printer. You might feel that your question has simply moved from the page to the mechanical printing device used to print the page. After all, the blankness of the page was caused by the defective counter, and an understanding of causes is usually sufficient explanation for their effects.

Out of desperation, you might finally decide to drive to the city where the printer was located and ask to examine the device responsible for the blank page. Upon examination, you discover that the device used to count the number of pages always misses this particular page in any book due to a defective gear in the counter. Examining the gear, you discover that a tooth has broken off as a result of normal wear. You return home satisfied that you understand the reason why the page is blank.

Of course, it would still be possible to pursue this line of questioning further. Why did *this* tooth break off and not some other? Why do the teeth break in the first place? And so on. At the end of this long line of questions will always be one that is unanswerable, like "Why is the structure of matter such that it can be formed into gears?" But scientific explanations generally stop far short of this point, having provided the desired level of explanation.

In this rather simple example, the explanation that is being sought is one that is described in terms of causes *inherent in the physical order of things;* these are causes that can usually be identified by empirical observation. It would be very simple to design experiments that would eventually lead to a complete scientific understanding of the process by which mechanical gears wear out and break under normal use. But suppose the blank page had been the result of an editorial decision. In this case, the discovery of the explanation would require an investigation into the purpose that existed in the mind of the editor. What kind of experiments could be designed to discover this purpose?

If the explanation requires the discovery of hidden purpose, then the investigation is not amenable to the usual methods of science. But purpose can frequently be as important an ingredient in a full explanation as a mechanical, chemical, or physical cause. In some cases, purpose is the most important component of an explanation. A question like "Why did Columbus sail to America?" should be answered by referring to his purpose in embarking on that adventure, not to the winds that blew on his sails.

The discovery of purpose is the domain of philosophy and theology. They have methods appropriate to this kind of investigation, which is substantially more complex than scientific investigations.[3] Conversely, these disciplines are not equipped to deal with the kind of causes with which the scientific method concerns itself. For theologians to suppose that they can put constraints on theories of origins based on their understanding of God's purposes in the creation is to suppose that the methods

---

3. Scientific explanations are widely misconstrued as very complicated just because they are frequently hard to understand. This difficulty is due to the mathematical language generally used to express scientific ideas—a language as foreign to most people as Latin. In reality, science, especially physics, tends to deal with incredibly simple problems—like the hydrogen atom, for example—that are much easier to study than problems like the causes of inflation, homelessness, schizophrenia, and so on. Although it sounds paradoxical, scientific explanations are simple, yet hard to understand.

of theology have a wider application than is justified. For scientists to suppose that they can determine God's purposes (or lack thereof) by an examination of the physical universe is to suppose that the methods of science have a wider application than is justified.

These considerations demonstrate the importance of distinguishing between the scientific method and theological method. It demonstrates that neither can be complete within itself as a full explanation of much of the natural world, and it also shows that the nature of their distinctive forms of explanation makes it impossible for them to contradict each other.

Theological and Scientific Explanations

The universe is filled with fascinating and wonderful things that call for explanation. One curious fact about the universe is that the majority of the atoms in the universe are hydrogen atoms. Why is hydrogen, the smallest and simplest of the atoms, also the most common? The most elementary answer that could be provided by a theological explanation without any additional information is that "God made more hydrogen atoms than any other kind because it was essential to His larger purpose in creating the universe." This answer would reflect the theological commitment that God is the sovereign Creator of the universe and that He has a larger plan into which the details must fit, even though some of those details may have no apparent explanation. This response is quite barren, amounting to little more than the empty assertion "that's the way it is." (But the theologian will do better in a moment, after he has some more information.)

On the other hand, the scientific explanation for the origin of the universe provides a very simple explanation in terms of physical laws. This explanation does not include a theological dimension because theology, properly understood, neither provides nor disputes explanations of this sort. If a theologian wanders into the research lab and engages the scientist in a discussion of such questions he ceases to be a theologian and becomes, instead, a poorly trained scientist.

According to current scientific theories, the universe began in an explosion that was initially so hot that there were no atoms at all, all matter being in a sort of molten state that was essentially pure energy. As the universe cooled, atoms were able to form from individual electrons and protons. Since hydrogen is the simplest atom, it forms the most rapidly. And that is why there are so many hydrogen atoms in the universe today. Simple. Science, it would appear, has explained why there are so many hydrogen atoms in the universe.

But this why is not the why of purpose, which is outside the domain of science and not amenable to the scientific method. To address the why of purpose the theologian needs to reenter the conversation. At this point, the theologian can do little more than repeat "That's the way that God did it." But with a little more insight from science, the theologian can do much better. (To paraphrase Einstein: Religion *with* science is *not* blind.)

Theologian: Why is there so much hydrogen in the universe?

Scientist: Because the initial conditions of the universe were very conducive to its production.

Theologian: What features of the universe are as they are because of this preponderance of hydrogen?

Scientist: Well, there are several. For one thing, hydrogen is the fuel that stars use to produce light. Without all this hydrogen, our sun could not shine; if the sun could not shine, then there could be no life. Hydrogen is also an important ingredient in water. The properties of water are so remarkable that many scientists feel that it is absolutely essential to life. So hydrogen has made the universe habitable for a number of reasons. Without hydrogen there would be no life in the universe.

Theologian: So the prevalence of hydrogen has made the universe habitable?

Scientist: For life as we know it, yes. In fact, for any kind of life of which we can even conceive, hydrogen would be essential.

Theologian: Why do you suppose the universe needs to be habitable?

Scientist: I have no idea. There is nothing within science to suggest that a habitable universe is any better than an uninhabitable one. I thought maybe *you* might be able to answer that question.

Theologian: Well, I would suggest that the presence of hydrogen in the universe in such large quantities indicates that God was concerned about the universe being habitable. His purposes involved the development of intelligent creatures, and this development was contingent upon the existence of a physically prepared universe. So the unusual initial conditions of the early universe could be the configuration installed by a Creator whose plan it was eventually to have people in the universe to have conversations like this one.

Scientist: Sounds good to me. I'm thirsty—how about a drink of water?

The fact that science does not use God as a part of its explanation for natural phenomenon is *not* an indication that science (or scientists) are against God or do not believe in Him. It is *not* an indication that scientists think God does not work in the universe. It is *not* an indication that scientists believe that everything can be explained without reference to God. It simply reflects the reality that stating "God did it" does not provide the kind of explanation sought for by the scientific method.

On the other hand, any truly complete explanation may indeed require the introduction of theological explanations in order to be complete. It is hard for science to address questions like "Why is there something rather than nothing?" or "Why is it that the universe seems to have been designed as a comfortable home for humans?"

Certain very important questions require the type of answer that can arise only out of a joint explanation provided by science and religion in dialogue with each other. One example of this is the anthropic principle, which is worth considering in some detail because of its clearly multidisciplinary nature.

The Anthropic Principle: Science and Religion in Dialogue?

Scientists do not like it when they cannot figure everything out. As much as they might be willing to admit privately that their theories are tentative, that they never have ultimate answers, that they are open to change, in practice they never give up searching for answers. As long as their curiosity is aroused, they will search.

It is thus very frustrating for science to develop a complicated theory, like quantum mechanics, and have it contain some elements that are apparently just arbitrary physical parameters, the values of which seem to be nothing more than brute facts. (A brute fact is something that just *is:* there is no way to explain it and it must simply be accepted as one of the givens in the physical situation.) The scientist examines his or her beautiful theory and continues to wonder about those few mysterious elements that he or she cannot quite explain—those brute facts.

One of the brute facts in the current theories of the universe is the ratio of the mass of the proton to that of the neutron. The neutron outweighs the proton by a fraction of a percent. This fact causes physicists no small amount of frustration. Why does the neutron have almost the same mass as the proton but not quite? Their masses are so close that there must be some reason for their proximity, just as two bullets imbedded side by side in the same tree would suggest that they were fired at the same spot. One could hardly argue that the two bullets have separate histories and are thus totally unrelated to each other, and it is only by coincidence that they happen to be imbedded in the same tree. In the same way, one can hardly argue that the neutron and proton masses are unrelated to each other; they are simply too close for such comfort. But why the small difference? As a scientific question, this "why" seems unanswerable: an arbitrary feature of the universe but one that has tremendous significance.

The curious small difference in the mass of the neutron and the proton is one of several important physical conditions that allow stars to shine for more than just a few hundred years. If the two masses were equal to one another, life could not exist in the universe, because stars could not shine long enough for life to "make it." This explanation—if it can be called that—appeals to a purpose. It says the neutron has slightly more mass than the proton because this condition is essential for the presence of life as we know it in the universe. But scientists are not sure whether this constitutes an explanation. It is certainly not an explanation of the traditional sort provided by science.

There are a number of such annoying features of the universe—things that seem to be just a certain very particular way for no apparent scientific reason: (1) The charge on the electron and the proton are exactly equal and opposite. How did these particles know that stable bodies such as ours could exist only if their charges were precisely equal and opposite? If this equality of electrical charges were compromised in any way, our bodies—indeed all the objects in the universe—would suddenly explode—not a happy prospect. (2) Elements heavier than hydrogen, like carbon and oxygen, are formed in the stars in a process that involves the perfect matchup of what should be unrelated energies. How did these energies know that the production of such heavy elements was crucial for life?

(3) Water has extraordinary properties that make it an almost magical liquid for living creatures. How did the atoms that make up water know that this particular combination was so important? (4) The sun shines at just the right color for chlorophyll molecules in plants to absorb the energy effectively. How does the sun know that the life of plants more than 90 million miles away is dependent upon its light? (5) The strong force that holds the nucleus together has exactly the right strength for the maintenance of the nuclear reactions that power the shining of the sun. How did the strong force know how strong it needed to be? (6) The initial conditions at the moment of the big bang—the temperature, density, and smoothness of the primordial "stuff"—were just right so that structures like suns with planets around them would eventually develop over the course of cosmic evolution. How did the big bang know to adjust its parameters so that the universe would eventually be habitable?

This list of apparent coincidences has a single thread linking them all together. That thread is life. Every single one of these apparently arbitrary physical facts must be exactly as it is, or there would be no life in the universe. The universe has "a fitness that hangs by a thread and that cries out for explanation."[4] The question is obvious: How did the universe come to

4. George Greenstein, *The Symbiotic Universe: Life and Mind in the Cosmos* (New York: William Morrow and Co., 1988), 240.

be so amazingly well designed for life, so finely tuned? If the smallest of details had been ever so slightly different during the very early stages of cosmic evolution, then the universe could never have become a place where people could ponder such questions. Minute changes in the values of a number of physical quantities would have led to a universe totally devoid of life.

Physicist George Greenstein responds to this question as follows:

> As we survey all the evidence, the thought insistently arises that some supernatural agency—or, rather, Agency—must be involved. Is it possible that suddenly, without intending to, we have stumbled upon scientific proof of the existence of a Supreme Being? Was it God who stepped in and so providentially crafted the cosmos for our benefit? Do we not see in its harmony, a harmony so perfectly fitted to our needs, evidence of what one religious writer has called "a preserving, a continuing, an intending mind; a Wisdom, Power, and Goodness far exceeding the limits of our thoughts"?[5]

This passage clearly demonstrates the apparently theological dimension of this apparently scientific problem. But Greenstein, in harmony with most physicists, rejects the possibility that there may be a theological explanation lurking behind the finely tuned universe. He prefers instead to hunt for the answer deep within quantum theory where there are suggestions that intelligent observers are necessary for physical reality to emerge from mere potentiality.[6]

---

5. Ibid., 27.

6. One of the deepest mysteries in physics relates to the problem of measurement in quantum theory. The theory seems to require that certain physical situations are not actually present in the universe until someone observes them. This paradox is often expressed in the example of Schrödinger's cat. (Schrödinger was one of the founders of quantum theory.) If a cat is placed in a box with some radioactive material that might decay and kill the cat, quantum theory predicts that the cat will go into a hybrid state that is half dead and half alive. When the box is opened to see how the cat is doing, it will immediately become either fully dead or fully alive, actualizing one of the possibilities latent in the former hybrid state. But, according to the standard interpretation of quantum theory, it stays in this hybrid state until it is observed.

This notion—observer created reality—is so difficult to accept that some people feel that quantum theory must be inadequate, not because there is anything wrong with it, but because it makes this extraordinary statement about systems that exist in hybrid states until observed. These hybrid states can be created in the laboratory and observed to respond in a way that is entirely analogous to Schrödinger's cat.

The hypothesis that the physical features of the universe are conditioned by the requirement that the universe must be capable of supporting life is called the anthropic principle. It is a controversial hypothesis tentatively embraced by some leading theoretical physicists as a powerful explanation, caustically criticized by other physicists as wishful anthropocentrism founded on poorly understood cosmological concepts, and admired from afar by theologians who wish desperately that it could be true.

The anthropic principle is perhaps the most profound idea in science today. It suggests that a remarkable array of physical parameters have had their numerical values selected by the requirement that the universe eventually bring forth life. If this is true, then our universe is surely far more interesting that we might ever have anticipated. If it is false, then science will have spent some time traveling down a most curious blind alley.

In either case, it would seem that there is reason for the scientist to consider making that long journey across the vast universe that now separates him or her from the theologians. And perhaps the theologians might open their tightly cloistered systematic theologies just a bit and let some of the light of science, however faint, shine in. And perhaps they will both be the wiser.

Conclusion

The anthropic principle is but one example of the kind of fruitful dialogue that could exist between science and religion if both would treat their methods as ploughshares capable of tilling the same soil. If dialogue could be perceived as something other than a prelude to an argument, if distant battles could be forgotten and recently buried hatchets left in the ground, then science and religion might be able to accomplish more together than they can apart.

There are countless ideas emerging from science, particularly physics, that are drawing scientists into a consideration of larger questions that once appeared to be the exclusive domain

---

Einstein died believing that quantum theory, which he helped create, must have something wrong with it, but nobody has been able to find any problems, though many of the best minds of this century have devoted their energies to the search.

of theology. Astronomer Adam Ford, who is also "priest in ordinary to the Queen at Chapel Royal, London," puts it like this:

> The practicing scientist nowadays may find it as reasonable to believe in God and to pray as it is to probe the atom or wrestle with a mathematical theorem. The days are gone when it was assumed that the pursuit of scientific method rules out the possibility of holding religious beliefs. These two areas of thought, once treated separately, now contribute jointly to a coherent and integrated vision of the world. Science and religion offer insights into one reality and together can build a framework of faith that encompasses the whole of contemporary life.[7]

Theoretical physicist Paul Davies argues that contemporary physical theories are drawing scientists ever closer to something at the heart of existence. Even though he is personally unsympathetic to organized religion, Davies is becoming convinced that there is *something* behind all of this, and he wonders if this something could be God. "It may seem bizarre," he argues in *God and the New Physics,* "but in my opinion science offers a surer path to God than religion. Right or wrong, the fact that science has actually advanced to the point where what were formerly religious questions can be seriously attacked itself indicates the far-reaching consequences of the new physics."[8]

We will conclude with a passage from John Polkinghorne, whose quote opened the chapter. Polkinghorne was a theoretical physicist whose studies of the physical universe led him ever deeper into theology until he felt led to become an Anglican priest. Polkinghorne is one of the leading advocates of the

---

7. Adam Ford, *Universe: God, Science and the Human Person* (Mystic, Conn.: Twenty-Third Publications, 1987), 11-12. In my opinion, Ford is exaggerating the extent to which science is moving scientists toward traditional religious activities, like praying to God. But it is certainly the case that abstract theological considerations are now of great interest to many physicists.

8. Paul Davies, *God and the New Physics* (New York: Simon and Schuster, 1983), ix. Davies is somewhat antagonistic toward traditional theology and is far more interested in the extent to which science might inform religion than vice versa. I would argue, however, that the very nature of the two disciplines would suggest that theology can make better use of scientific ideas than science could make of theological ideas. This is due, of course, to the much larger breadth of theology and its need to be informed on a broad front. Science has a much narrower focus than theology.

need for science and religion to communicate more effectively
with each other.

Science and theology have encountered each other in
a way that seems, to me at least, to be characterized by
fruitful interaction rather than mutual friction. Einstein
once said, "Religion without science is blind. Science
without religion is lame." His instinct that they need each
other was right, though I would not describe their separate shortcomings in quite the terms he chose. Rather I
would say, "Religion without science is confined; it fails
to be completely open to reality. Science without religion
is incomplete; it fails to attain the deepest possible understanding." The remarkable insights that science affords
us into the intelligible workings of the world cry out for
an explanation more profound than that which itself can
provide. Religion, if it is to take seriously its claim that
the world is the creation of God, must be humble enough
to learn from science what that world is actually like. The
dialogue between them can only be mutually enriching.
The scientist will find in theology a unifying principle
more fundamental than the grandest unified field theory.
The theologian will encounter in science's account of the
pattern and structure of the physical world a reality
which calls forth his admiration and wonder. Together
they can say with the psalmist:

O Lord, how manifold are thy works! in wisdom
thou hast made them all [Ps. 104:24, KJV].[9]

---

9. Polkinghorne, *Science and Creation: The Search for Understanding*, 97-98. Reprinted
with permission of SPCK (Society for Promoting Christian Knowledge) Publishing,
London. Polkinghorne is one of the leaders of what seems to be a growing contingent of
British physicists who are engaging in meaningful theological discussion. Their enthusiasm is not yet shared by their colleagues in the New World.

11

A Marriage Made in Heaven

• • • • •

The very beauty of form in all that is visible, proclaim, however silently, both that the world was created and also that its Creator could be none other than God whose greatness and beauty are both ineffable and invisible.

Augustine

I want to know how God created this world. I am not interested in this or that phenomenon, in the spectrum of this or that element. I want to know His thoughts, the rest are details.

Albert Einstein

• • • • •

The Parable of the Rainbow

They met at twilight, just as the sun was about to go down. The location was unimpressive save for a beautiful rainbow that arched across the sky, its colors more vivid than any of them had ever seen. The five weary travelers had come from different continents, different centuries, different cultures to stand here together and appreciate this rainbow.

For a few moments they wondered why they were here; they didn't know each other and didn't even all speak the same language. Each wondered about the odd manner of dress adopted by the others. But their purpose soon became clear as they discovered a scroll at their feet with their names on it. They picked up their scrolls and read the instructions: "You have been selected as representatives of the finest thinkers ever to wonder about the universe. On the scroll before you, write your reactions to the beautiful rainbow in front of you in the form of questions. These questions will be answered and will become the description of the rainbow."

After some thought, each of them began to write.

The scientist wrote, "Why do the colors of the rainbow separate into the pattern I see here? Why is the rainbow arched as if a portion of a great circle? Why do rainbows appear only after a rainfall?"

The philosopher wrote, "What is the nature of the beauty in this rainbow? Does it have a separate existence like trees and flowers? How does the beauty of this rainbow relate to the beauty of a sunset, a poem, a child?"

The theologian wrote, "Does this feeling of peace I find in this scene originate in God? Am I worshiping God as I stand here appreciating this beautiful scene?"

The artist wrote, "What is the essence of these colors? Would it be possible to create a painting of this scene that would evoke the same appreciation? What is it about these particular colors that makes this so beautiful?"

The musician wrote, "Can I duplicate this feeling of beauty with music? Is there a way to make a blind person appreciate this scene by somehow capturing its tranquillity in music?"

The scrolls were collected, and they waited together for their answers. They found themselves able to talk to one another and began to discuss the questions they had formulated. Each of them believed his questions about the rainbow were the most fundamental. Each of them was convinced that when the scrolls were returned, the others would see that their questions about the rainbow were either superficial or irrelevant.

The scientist was particularly, even obnoxiously, insistent that the rainbow was nothing but water droplets with sun shining through them and that any emotional response to the rainbow was superficial. He pointed out that if the water droplets were removed there would be no more rainbow. The philosopher, who was hard to understand, argued that the scientist was not looking at the rainbow as a whole and was mistaken if he thought it could be described as nothing but a collection of water droplets. He seemed to be insisting that "wholes are more than collections of parts."

The theologian, who spoke in parables, countered with remarkable confidence that both the scientist and the philosopher were wrong in even considering the rainbow as the significant object; he argued that the feeling of transcendence, of worship, of transport was the important aspect. The artist and the musician felt the emotion generated within each of the observers by the rainbow was the important aspect. They argued that the real significance was the human response to the rainbow, not its internal structure or philosophical significance.

The five thinkers waited eagerly for the return of the scrolls. The theologian opened his first and read the following: "You are to be congratulated on the profound questions you have asked about the rainbow. It is clear that you understand the rainbow. The feeling of worship in your soul does indeed come from God; the beauty of the rainbow is one of the windows through which you can look beyond the creation and see the Creator."

Feeling rather pleased at this affirmation of his questions, the theologian waited for the others to open their scrolls so that they would see that their perspectives had been misguided and that they would need to take back the unkind things they had said about theology. But to his surprise, every scroll started with the same complimentary affirmation: "You are to be congratulated on the profound questions you have asked about the rainbow. *It is clear that you understand the rainbow.*"

Each scroll then proceeded to affirm the specific questions asked, stating that those questions indeed were at the heart of understanding the rainbow. No one's questions were considered to be irrelevant or more fundamental than any others. Somehow they had all asked the right questions. Somehow the rainbow had all of these different dimensions, and none was any more important than the others.

So each of the thinkers agreed to exchange scrolls, realizing that their one-dimensional perspective on the rainbow had been robbing them of a full understanding of its richness. And as they spent time with the scrolls that were not their own, their appreciation for the rainbow grew until it became an object of much wonder.

Outline

It is one of the tragedies of our time that science and religion, our two great systems of thought, the two defining characteristics of our Western worldview, find themselves isolated from each other through mutual misunderstanding and the accidents of history. We have argued in this book that religion and science need each other, for they are the twin lights that mark the path of our modern world.

In this chapter we will return to the argument of the first chapter: an adequate worldview must recognize the authority of both science and religion. We will argue, as a summation of the material in the previous chapter, that religion is the only legitimate source for explanations about the purposes that exist in our big universe and that science is the only legitimate source for explanations about the empirical dimensions of our natural world. The universe cannot be molded into the form that religion would like it to have, so that religious or biblical truths can be found in the details of the created order; and the purposes that religion may discover in this created order cannot be argued out of existence by scientists whose methods are not adequate for finding such purposes.

These two aspects of the world—description and purpose—are distinct and studied by different methods. A mature worldview recognizes this distinction.

Worldviews Are Multidimensional

There are many questions at the heart of a worldview. In general, they fall naturally into two broad categories—(1) *Descriptive:* What is the world? What is it made of? How is it arranged? How do I feel about this arrangement (what is my subjective psychological reaction)? How do changes take place? How do I respond to those changes? (2) *Purposive:* Why is there a world at all? How do I fit into this world? How should I live in this world? Did God make this world?

The first category of questions considers the details of the world, details of interest to the various scientific disciplines, from physics to psychology. It is a reductionistic approach that attempts to explain complex phenomena in terms of simpler, better-understood components. It attempts to explain rainbows, for example, in terms of water droplets. The second category considers the meaning of those details. It is a holistic approach that attempts to understand how those details relate to the larger whole of which they are a part, a larger whole that includes the person asking the question. It explains rainbows, in this example, in terms of beauty.

The first category asks: What? where? when? and how?—What are rainbows? Where do we find them? When do they appear? How are they produced? These are the kinds of questions science can answer: Rainbows ares optical effects created by the refraction of light. We find them in the sky. They appear after rainfall. They are produced by sunlight refracting through droplets of water.

The second category of question asks: Why? Why are there rainbows? Why are they beautiful? The fallacy of scientific materialism is in its assumption that why questions are already answered in the what, when, where, and how. But the scientist cannot explain the extraordinary emotion that is the response to beauty. This explanation does not find itself in the evolutionary origins of the human race. It is an independent category of explanation that requires a much larger perspective to understand. The Judeo-Christian tradition has long understood that beauty[1] comes from God, "from whom all blessings flow."

These categories of explanation are independent, because they are striving to accomplish different objectives. The descriptive approach tries to remove the mystery from nature by reducing all complex phenomena to the point in which it becomes nothing but the sterile activity of tiny components, operating without purpose or direction, blindly following a few elementary laws of physics. By contrast, the purposive approach focus-

---

1. Beauty is one of the "Six Great Ideas" on which philosopher Mortimer Adler expounded in his book and the public television series of the same name. In the book he concedes that beauty remains one of the most difficult of the timeless philosophical concepts. He challenges the reader to "say what is common to—what universal qualities are present in—the admirable beauty of a prize-winning rose, Beethoven's Kreutzer Sonata, a triple play in the ninth inning of a baseball game, Michelangelo's *Pieta*, a Zen garden, Milton's sonnet on his blindness, a display of fireworks," and, we should add, a rainbow. See Mortimer Adler, *Six Great Ideas* (New York: Macmillan Publishing Co., 1981), 122.

es directly on the mystery, trying to discover the large patterns invisible from the perspective of the details.

Consider the example of a picture on a television screen. At one level, that of the details, it consists of nothing but a special screen that glows when it is struck by electrons shot from a gun at the back of the television screen. A scientist might attempt to understand the production of a television image by analyzing the electrons that are hitting the screen, studying the response of the screen to the impact of the electrons, describing the light that is emitted from the screen after the electron impact. This is certainly one level of explanation relevant to a television set. But this type of analysis, focused as it is on the smallest components of the larger whole, will never be able to see the "picture."

At a much higher level of analysis, the television screen might be displaying the flight of an eagle as it soars majestically above an open field, searching for prey. This scene from nature could be described as "awe inspiring" or "beautiful," words that would not be used, at least by the nonscientist, to describe the phenomenon from the perspective of the electrons and the television screen. There are at least two levels of explanation here. One says that the phenomenon is the bombardment of a television screen with electrons. The other says that the phenomenon is a picture of an eagle soaring in the sky above a beautiful field. The two explanations are clearly different. Is one right and one wrong?

Mature Worldviews

One of the measures of the maturity of a worldview is the extent to which these two categories of questions have been separated and recognized as independent. In primitive societies there is no such separation. The details and the meaning of those details are bound inextricably together.

We can see this in the worldview described in the famous poem *The Song of Hiawatha* by Henry Wadsworth Longfellow, which describes the rather romantic way certain native Americans viewed the world around them. In this epic poem, full of authentic Indian mythology, customs, and folklore, we find the wise old Nokomis answering questions posed by the young Hiawatha about the world around him. The answers reflect the worldview of Nokomis, in which everything has a purpose. Nothing is just a detail.

> By the shore of Gitche Gumee,
> By the shining Big-Sea-Water,
> Stood the wigwam of Nokomis,
> Daughter of the Moon, Nokomis.

> * * *

> There the wrinkled, old Nokomis
> Nursed the little Hiawatha
> Rocked him in his linden cradle
> Bedded soft in moss and rushes.

> * * *

> Many things Nokomis taught him
> Of the stars that shine in heaven . . .
> Showed the broad white road in heaven
> Pathway of the ghosts, the shadows
> Running straight across the heavens
> Crowded with the ghosts, the shadows.
> Saw the rainbow in the heaven
> In the eastern sky the rainbow
> Whispered: what is that, Nokomis?

> * * *

> And the good Nokomis answered
> Tis the heaven of flowers you see there;
> All the wild flowers of the forest
> All the lilies of the prairie
> When on earth they fade and perish
> Blossom in that heaven above us.[2]

In this excerpt we can see Nokomis explaining the Milky Way (the broad, white road in heaven) as the heavenly abode of the ghosts, the shadows of people who once lived on the earth. The Milky Way is a road "crowded with the ghosts" as they make their way in the world to come. Nokomis explains the col-

---

2. Henry Wadsworth Longfellow, *The Song of Hiawatha*, in *Hiawatha* (Milwaukee: Raintree Publications, 1984), 3-7.

ors of the rainbow as derived from the colors of the wildflowers on the earth. Wildflowers lose their beauty and die, but their death is not in vain, for their colors migrate to the rainbow, to be enjoyed again and again.

In these kinds of explanations we see the union of detail and meaning. Nokomis' answers explain, in a primitive way, *what* the colors of the rainbow are. But more important, they explain *why* the rainbow is there. This kind of tangled, subjective explanation is characteristic of primitive worldviews. The universe has no separate existence to be studied apart from the meaning ascribed to it by the primitive explanations.

We see this same kind of explanation for the rainbow expressed in the Genesis account of the great Flood. God set the rainbow in the heaven as a sign that He would never again destroy the world in a flood. And to a prescientific culture, this was more than adequate to answer any "why" questions about rainbows.

Neither of these explanations does much with the actual details of the rainbow. Hiawatha's rainbow gets its color from wildflowers by an unstated mechanism of no interest to Hiawatha; Noah's rainbow gets its colors from God by some equally unknown process. But both explanations serve to evoke a certain reverence and appreciation for the rainbow. By contrast, the rainbow as described by modern science is simply a large collection of water droplets through which sunlight is refracting. In the scientific explanation, it is not something to be reverenced; it is just a "detail."[3]

The rainbow, like the television picture, can be understood on two levels: (1) On the level of the details it is described scientifically in terms of the laws of physics. Light from the sun is refracted by water droplets in such a way that each of the constituent colors of the visible spectrum can be independently discerned. This explanation does not inspire reverence for the

---

3. It should be pointed out that scientifically literate people find a certain beauty in the underlying natural laws responsible for phenomenon. While the explanations provided by science may seem at first to sterilize the phenomenon under consideration, the reverence creeps back in as another profound layer of mystery manifests itself in the symmetry, beauty, and elegance of the physical theories. It is here that many scientists, such as Einstein, experience what they interpret to be an essentially religious response.

rainbow. In fact, it would probably lessen the appreciation many people have for rainbows! (2) At the level of purpose, the rainbow can serve a number of functions. Personally, I find a rainbow to be so beautiful that I generally try to pause and soak in the beauty for a moment. I find myself moved to praise the Creator for this type of very special interaction between myself as a creature and the rainbow as a part of the creation. And I constantly wonder about the nature of beauty. Why is it that the rainbow is so beautiful? Why is it that it moves us mere mortals? In the big picture there is a fundamental relationship between the creature and the creation, a relationship that cannot be uncovered by poking around inside the atoms and molecules of our existence.

The Fallacy of the One-Dimensional Worldview

One of the lessons of history, sketchily outlined in the preceding chapters, is that a worldview cannot be constructed from a single perspective. We saw the theologians of the Early Church struggling to assemble the details of the physical universe by trying to find that information in the Bible. We saw the scientific materialists struggling to find meaning in the universe as they searched in vain within those very same physical details. Neither was successful. The Early Church theologians never discovered the physical universe in the Bible. The scientific materialists never discovered the purpose of existence in the laws of nature.

In the three chapters devoted to creationism, we considered the scientific creationists' attempt to reorganize modern science and return to the approach of the Early Church as they attempted to discover the details of the physical universe in the pages of the Bible.

In the language of this chapter, we would say that the world must be viewed from two complementary perspectives: that of detail and that of purpose. To see clearly we must look through binoculars—not telescopes. We need perspective and depth, not merely detail. And yet we still find scholars trying to view the world with one eye closed, as if unaware that the perception of depth requires that both eyes be opened.

Adherents to the modern creationist movement are trying to make the details of the creation conform to preconceived concepts drawn from religious convictions. Because of these preconceived notions about the purpose of the biblical record, they find it necessary to deny the conclusions of modern science. Their message is clear: The authority of science must be subordinated to that of the Bible, even though there is absolutely no reason to believe the Bible was ever meant to be a source for science.

In the same way, adherents to scientific materialism are trying to make the purpose (or the lack of purpose) of creation conform to their preconceived concepts drawn from scientific convictions. Their message is also clear: Science is the only means to uncover truth, and, since science has not discovered God, He must not exist, or He must be undiscoverable (unknowable). This they confidently assert, though it has never been established that the methods of science are adequate to discover God.

The contribution that the Bible makes to the worldview of the Christian is to infuse deep meaning into the apparently sterile details discovered by science. Knowing that the God we worship created these small details should make us interested in these details, just as a boring house may become a structure of great interest when it is discovered that some famous architect built it. While we may find the house itself uninteresting, our great fascination with the architect leads us to examine the house closely, to see what we can learn about its famous designer.

The universe is the house designed and built by God. The Christian should rejoice with each new scientific discovery, because it sheds a little more light on the details of God's creation. If we claim to be truly interested in the Creator, we should demonstrate some interest in His creation. Surely knowledge of the creation must contribute to a knowledge of the Creator. The founders of modern science—Copernicus, Kepler, Galileo, and Newton—all felt their science brought them closer to their God. And many contemporary scientists are rediscovering this theological dimension of their scientific endeavors.

The modern Christian should thus be eager to learn of the discoveries of science. If the big bang theory is demonstrated to be correct, then we should embrace it and marvel at the interesting way God chose to bring the universe into existence. If biological evolution should be demonstrated to be correct, then we should embrace it and marvel at the interesting way God chose to bring us into existence. However old the earth may be, however it may have developed, we are still its stewards. However old the human race may be, however it may have developed, we still exist in the image of God.

These are important affirmations that transcend the steadily improving descriptions of the universe that science is providing. God can be affirmed as our Creator and our Father independently of how the universe developed or how we came to have the form we do. The image of God does not disappear from Homo sapiens if they acquire an evolutionary origin, just as a child's innocence does not disappear when the child finds out he or she is adopted. Similarly, God remains immanent in the creation, even though the description of that creation may change.

Modern science desperately needs the infusion of meaning that can be provided by religion. The Church of Jesus Christ does not exist on a separate planet from that of modern science. We live in the same world, we observe the same universe, and we need the same gospel. Modern science gropes blindly for the meaning that can be provided only by a true appreciation of God the Creator. But the conservative church, to the extent that it has heeded the voice of the scientific creationists, has withheld that meaning from science by insisting on a particular description of the universe, one that cannot be embraced by most scientists. So many scientists struggle to find purpose, searching with their one scientific eye for a depth that can be discovered only with two eyes.

Carl Sagan, the flamboyant astronomer from Cornell University, claims, "The Cosmos is all that is, ever was, or ever will be,"[4] as if science has somehow convinced him that God does not exist. Isaac Asimov, popular author of more than 400 books, claims, "The scientific view sees the Universe as following its

---

4. Carl Sagan, *Cosmos* (New York: Random House, 1980), 4.

own rules blindly, without either interference or direction,"[5] as if science has convinced him that there is no purpose in the universe.

Peter Atkins, a chemist from Oxford, describes his own existence as that of an intelligent elephant: "Man and his counterparts elsewhere are merely elephants with a tendency to hubris. We are fragments of the universe, elephants happily free to roam intellectually as well as spatially. As elaborate outcrops of the physical world, and no more than that we are no more necessary to its existence than is a breeze."[6] Richard Dawkins, the prominent Oxford biologist, named his last book *The Blind Watchmaker: Why the Evidence of Evolution Reveals a Universe Without Design*. Dawkins argues, unsuccessfully in my opinion, that science has shown that the world has no "Mind" behind it.[7] Edward Wilson, the controversial sociobiologist from Harvard, suggests that the natural human tendency toward religion finds its origin in evolutionary history. He suggests that religion can survive only if it stops worshiping God and starts worshiping "the evolutionary epic."[8]

The story of Edward Wilson points up the tragedy of the unholy war between science and religion. Wilson, one of the most important scientists living today, was raised in a Southern Baptist church and as a teenager had a strong religious commitment. But he had been taught to believe that one had to make a choice between evolution and God, that they are irreconcilable enemies. So when he began to study biology and became convinced that evolution was true, he was forced to discard his faith. His worldview was not big enough for both of them. Who knows how many prominent scientists have had their faith destroyed because they were raised to believe, or convinced in

---

5. Isaac Asimov, *In the Beginning* (New York: Pantheon, 1983), 11.

6. Peter Atkins, *The Creation* (San Francisco: W. H. Freeman and Co., 1981), vii.

7. Richard Dawkins, *The Blind Watchmaker: Why the Evidence of Evolution Reveals a Universe Without Design* (New York: W. W. Norton, 1986). On the back cover of this book, Isaac Asimov comments, "A lovely book. Original and lively, it expounds the ins and outs of evolution with enthusiastic clarity, answering, at every point, *the cavemen of creationism*." (Emphasis added.)

8. Robert Wright, *Three Scientists and Their Gods* (New York: Times Books, 1988), 190.

some other way, that modern science was an enemy of the Christian faith? The Church cannot afford to put so large a distance between itself and modern science.

This could be a long list. The worldview of modern science, which is characterized by its extraordinary ability to explain so many aspects of the natural world, is remarkable for the very difficulty that it encounters in explaining why science is such a meaningful endeavor.

Where Do We Go from Here?

The Church of Jesus Christ must take care to distance itself from unnecessary conflict with modern science. When science is properly understood, it becomes clear it can pose no challenge to religion. And when scientists and science writers are properly restrained, they will stop writing as if to challenge religion. No theory of cosmic expansion, particle decay, natural selection, continental drift, and so forth, can ever contradict the Christian faith.

In the same way, when religion is properly understood, it becomes clear it can pose no challenge to science. And when Christian writers are properly restrained, they will stop writing as if to challenge science. No religious doctrines need ever come in conflict with modern science.

The contemporary Christian must learn to accept and become comfortable with the results of modern science. It is dishonest to check oneself into a hospital expecting that modern science will be able to cure you—and then to march out and demand that modern science be removed from high school textbooks. There is no conspiracy within science to destroy religion. There are only a few outspoken scientists who have an antagonism toward religion that they occasionally express.

The Church cannot tie its gospel to a long-discarded science and expect people to take it seriously. Our theology *must* be distinguished from our scientific description of the world. We must always be quick to affirm that God is the Creator, but we must not suggest that this creation could have been accomplished in only one particular way; that explanation must be left to science. Creation must be understood as the theological dimension of the larger explanation provided for the riddle of our existence.

Only in this way can the conflict between science and religion be avoided and the gospel allowed to move freely, unfettered by the chains it has been forced to drag around in the past.

INDEX